CONCILIUM

concilium

1990/4

COLLEGIALITY
PUT TO THE TEST

Edited by

James Provost and
Knut Walf

SCM Press · London
Trinity Press International · Philadelphia

August 1990

ISBN: 0 334 03003 x

Typeset at The Spartan Press Ltd, Lymington, Hants
Printed by Dotesios Printers Ltd, Trowbridge, Wilts

Concilium: Published February, April, June, August, October, December.

For the best and promptest service, new subscribers should apply as follows:

US and Canadian subscribers:

Trinity Press International, 3725 Chestnut Street, Philadelphia PA 19104
Fax: 215–387–8805

UK and other subscribers:

SCM Press, 26–30 Tottenham Road, London N1 4BZ
Fax: 071–249–3776

Existing subscribers should direct any queries about their subscriptions as above.

Subscriptions rates are as follows:

United States and Canada: $59.95
United Kingdom, Europe, the rest of the world (surface): £34.95
Airmail to countries outside Europe: £44.95

Further copies of this issue and copies of most back issues of *Concilium* are available at $12.95 (US and Canada)/£6.95 rest of the world.

Contents

Editorial

Its teaching on the collegiality of bishops was a major contribution of the Second Vatican Council. In an effort to complete the work of Vatican I and to balance an over-emphasis on papal primacy, the council sought to restore the proper relationship of bishops with their head, the successor of Peter, in episcopal service to the Church.

The initial fruits of this conciliar insight are evident. Even during the council itself, and clearly since then, the collegiality of bishops has supported many developments in the structures and in the lived experience of the Church. The collegial solicitude of bishops for needy areas of the Church has led to a sharing of personnel and material resources, and especially to a sensitivity to the condition of Christians in various parts of the world where they are in need or under tension and oppression. The structures which express this solicitude have themselves matured since their affirmation or encouragement during the council; national and international bishops' conferences, the synod of bishops, various other synodal experiences of a national or regional scope. These have engaged in a variety of apostolic efforts, ranging from important pastoral letters and decisions concerning the prayer and worship of the Church, to decisions on various disciplinary issues which affect the life of the local churches.

In more recent years, however, there appears to be a hesitation in certain quarters, some of them highly placed, with regard to the collegiality of bishops. There are tendencies to restrict its significance, to weaken its structural expressions, and to question the very meaning of collegiality itself. It is as if the balance which the Second Vatican Council sought to restore in the Church is itself being questioned, whether in the name of a reemphasized papal centralism or a breakdown of catholic communion altogether.

This is not an altogether unexpected stage in the process of receiving the conciliar training. Any major council which has worked for reform in the Church has undergone a period of hesitation and resistance, especially as the bishops who attended the council are replaced by men who were trained before the council and did not go through the conciliar experience itself. Chalcedon, Lateran IV, Trent – all knew such a period following the close of the council itself. The proof of the value of a council's teaching is its ability to outlive those who attended the council itself, and to take root in the life of the Church for subsequent generations.

So it should not be surprising that 'collegiality' is now being put to the test. This indeed is a time to test the conciliar teaching, to see if it does represent a significant insight into the nature of the Church which deserves practical expression in the very structures of hierarchical authority. But the test is not one of influence and prestige, intrigue and political manoeuvring; it must be a test of the gospel, of whether this teaching truly is of the Spirit. To assess collegiality in this fashion, it must be placed in the context of the mission of the Church, not just its political life; to evaluate the value of the conciliar teaching on collegiality, it must be judged by its fruits, not just by its friends or enemies.

As we approach the third millennium, the Church is faced with the task of evangelization on a world-wide scale and with a renewed intensity. Every portion of the globe is affected. No longer are there strictly 'missionary lands' and fully 'Catholic nations'. Evangelization is required in each place, among all peoples, even those with a long Christian tradition.

But this is not all. Not only is the number of people increasing, but increased numbers of peoples are aware of their own dignity, culture and density. The gospel must become for them the 'good news' which Christ intended for all peoples, but more and more this cannot be done if the gospel comes to them as something so limited by a particular cultural history and expression that it cannot be grasped as truly their 'own'.

It is in this context of mission that collegiality – and the Catholic Church itself – is being put to the test today. The contemporary challenge of mission calls for effective approaches of evangelization in settings which are more extensive than local dioceses, but more restricted and specific than can be addressed from a universal perspective. The Church needs an increasingly effective collegiality to support its unity as well as its appropriate diversity in carrying out this mission.

How is the Church measuring up? To what extent is collegiality surviving the test? It is too soon to tell, and we are too close to the experience to be able to provide a fully objective evaluation. Yet we can obtain some preliminary indications, we are able to discern some of the initial results of the test to which collegiality is being put. So in this volume we have asked knowledgeable scholars and experts in the life of the Church to issue an initial report card, evaluating how collegiality is doing so far, in these twenty-five years since the close of Vatican II.

Our report is divided into three sections: theory, structures, and practice. A brief word about each may help to grasp the overall impression which is verified only by a careful reading of these papers.

The theory of collegiality in its contemporary expression is found in Vatican II. But there are many readings of Vatican II today. Herwi Rikhof takes us back to the texts of *Lumen Gentium* 23–25 which are central to understanding the conciliar teaching, and explores both the development of the texts themselves and, more significantly, the intention which is evident in the drafting process.

The theory itself has been put to the test explicitly by the two extraordinary meetings of the Synod of Bishops, the first in 1969 and the latest in 1985. Jan Grootaers explores how these collegial bodies tried to understand the meaning of collegiality itself. It is clear that the divisions which were evident during the council have not disappeared, but the synodal meetings themselves evidence the value of collegiality to some extent.

The theory of collegiality continues to be evident in a variety of ways. Three of these are explored in our studies. Donato Valentini explores the writings of theologians to develop an understanding of the major contemporary theological views about the theory of collegiality. Remigiusz Sobański uses official church documents issued since the council to seek an understanding of what, from a canonical perspective, the theory of collegiality means. Heiner Grote presents yet another perspective, that of a scholar who examines the Catholic understanding of collegiality from the prospective of a Reformed Christian in Europe.

Four studies explore the structural expression of collegiality in the Church twenty-five years after Vatican II. Ludwig Kaufmann takes a critical look at the development of the Synod of Bishops, especially in the light of the expectations which led to its creation during Vatican II. Peter Leisching explores the debate about the nature of bishops' conferences as a structure rooted in collegiality. Joseph Hajjar, from the perspective of Eastern Catholic Churches, examines what the 'Patriarchal Synods' in the proposals for a new Eastern Code of Canon Law really mean. Pasquale Colella concludes this section with some considerations on the current law relative to the selection of bishops.

What is the overall impression regarding the structures of collegiality? Mixed – there seems to be more hesitation to implement collegial structures than would be warranted by the degree of consensus that does exist about the basic theory, even with all the diversities that are present there.

Finally, five authors turn to the practical experience of collegiality in the Church today, examining in turn the North and South American experiences, Europe, Asia and Africa. A general impression from these studies is that collegiality is being understood as important to the evangelization of the nations, primarily through bishops' conferences.

Thomas Reese focuses on the development of the National Conference of Catholic Bishops as a case study of collegiality in action within the United States. Gervásio Fernandes de Queiroga reviews the history of the Brazilian bishops' conference, pointing to successes and stresses in opting for the poor and seeking to assess the impact of violence and domination.

Luc de Fleurquin traces the development of the Council of Episcopal Conferences of Europe, a multi-national group which is faced today with the situation of the new Europe. Julio X. Labayen reports on another inter-conference organization, the Federation of Asian Bishops' Conferences, which is working to promote evangelization in an entirely different context. Antoine Matenkadi Finifini examines the expression of collegiality in the African situation, with special attention to efforts to call an African council, now termed an African 'synod'.

Overall, our report indicates a mixed reception of collegiality to date. As indicated earlier, this is not unexpected. There are several encouraging signs, however, that the commitment of the post-conciliar generations to collegiality is real and deep; it is not being discouraged by the expected 'testing' of collegiality, but rather in many quarters is strengthening and maturing. But only the experience of the next twenty-five years will tell the extent to which these hopes are justified.

James Provost
Knut Walf

Beyond Marxism

A wave of liberation is sweeping through the world, and it has not yet begun to ebb. In Eastern Europe, Latin America and Africa, long-defended totalitarian positions have finally fallen. In many places political Marxism, which also determined social and economic conditions, has come to an end. This appears to be no temporary retreat; in fact we seem to have come to the end of a period in history which was deeply marked by Marxism and the opposition which it provoked. A final judgment cannot be made until the process has run its course, and that may still take years. One thinks of the stagnation in Romania, Bulgaria and Albania, and above all also in China, North Korea and Cuba.

However, the historical developments in the Soviet Union and the countries of Eastern Europe, Latin America and Africa need to be pondered deeply by Christians. Generalizations and clichés are not enough when ideological and political positions, long-established and entrenched, and even defended by force, are being dealt with so radically before our eyes. What is taking place in these countries represents a challenge to Christians to make a thorough investigation of the ideological context of their existence. The contrasts between Marxism and liberalism, between two views of life and the world and the social and political forms associated with them, are emerging more clearly than ever before. That these critical movements in Europe, with its long history, are also being reflected in Africa and Latin America, once again underlines the importance of thorough reflection on 'Western' values and the social and political systems associated with them.

It is not difficult to outline in a few points the sharp contrasts which existed between 'East' and 'West' until quite recently. Usually they are described as freedom and democracy on 'our' side and totalitarian state control and party dictatorship on 'their' side. When it seemed that the pressure could no longer be maintained – for whatever reasons – the West called on the peoples and governments of the Eastern European countries to make the Western value of freedom the focal point of the reforms that were wanted: freedom of movement and travel, freedom of information and expression of opinion, freedom of social and political organization, a free market economy. If these freedoms are realized to the full and are made the basic principles of the 'new order', the result will be an ideological and political pluralism, decentralization of the control of ideas and power, a relaxation of the totalitarian grip on internal national and cultural contrasts, in other words, the introduction of the democratic order into society. Moreover everyone feels that the reintegration of the systems which are now breaking apart into new cultural, social and political units will be a very long-drawn-out process.

So questions of interest to Christians are: around what values will this reintegration take place? What consensus of values can come about which will inspire the construction of a new society? What will keep people together when the totalitarian authority of party and bureaucracy, of the military and political apparatus, drops away or is reduced to dimensions which the new democrats can accept? What role will the church societies be able to play in the building up of this new society? The Roman Catholic church in Poland and the Protestant churches in the German Democratic Republic were closely involved in the critical movements. But what will this relationship be when these movements can exist in the free field of a Western-style secularized democratic pluralism?

Christians who live in a 'Western' context have to ask: what has the West to offer in these circumstances? How will the construction of a society worth living in actually be achieved? What are we to expect for Europe after 1992? And can that be an inspiring model for the countries of Eastern Europe, in Africa, in Asia and in Latin America?

The questions raised here can be reduced to just one question, which takes this form: are freedom and democracy values with a particular content, or are they no more than formal principles depending on the type of society that people want to bring about?

Many analyses give one the impression that in the West the last-mentioned view is the dominant one. The freedom that is praised is largely seen as a formal, non-ideological principle, without any content. However, the international swing which previously Marxist countries are now making towards a market-orientated economy also seem to be prompted by a different set of values. The bankruptcy of Marxism as a truth-system – in accordance with the criteria of Marxism as society – emerged from the total and disastrous inadequacies of economic, social and cultural praxis. And this experience led to a shift in the evaluation of the system on which the society was constructed. It brought the populace out on the streets in large numbers, in protest against the party dictatorship. Given the outcome of the elections, the ideas of the intelligentsia about a third way between capitalism and Communism, in the form of a reformed state socialism, also seem likely to be rejected. There is a desire to be citizens in the 'Western' sense: individuals who can live their lives with worth and responsibility on the basis of human rights, in a state with a liberal constitution, with power-sharing and a parliamentary democracy, in relative prosperity, a democracy which devotes itself openly and internationally to the universal values of peace, justice and the integrity of creation.

However, the way which must be taken to achieve that is marked by the need for rapid industrialization, economic growth and modernization, the cleaning-up of a polluted environment, and an acceptable means of incorporation into an integral European security system. In this complex transitional situation, how will the young democracies go about the sought-for reorientation of values? The practice of politics must not be based solely on the technology of power; at the same time people must be put in a position of being able to realize the values mentioned above as a content of their life, without their options again being narrowed by ideology and politics.

What role can the churches play here? The answer is by no means evident. And Pope John-Paul II has rightly seen here material for a special Synod of Bishops (a Eurosynod). Can the churches in these countries be more than the guardians of moral norms and values? In post-Marxist civic life can they find a new public presence? How will they react to the 'secularization' which they so fear, the great enemy in the West? With intolerance, criticism and fanaticism? With a renewed identification of church and nation? And where will these nations find something to bind them together? How will the churches react to the regional independence for minority states and ethnic groupings which is wanted? No group may any longer *a priori* be regarded as an enemy unless it is intolerant and seeks to break up a social order orientated on consensus for the sake of one all-dominating truth. The arena has become pluralistic: that is what people want. In that case, what have the churches to learn from the 'Western' churches, which have already for so long existed in a liberal social order, without accepting it in principle until well into the twentieth century, either politically or in terms of its economic and political programme? This is a question which can be put to both worlds: how can the Christian churches stretch out their hands to the universal humanism which will (have to) be the ethical basis for European society?

All this also affects conditions within the church. The church society which has come into being under pressure in the countries of the Eastern bloc will cease to exist. Religious individualization will increase along with social individualization. And again one may ask: how will the churches react? Free individuals, who have access to a wide range of information about the world, will have to find the basis for their Christian commitment in their own well-formed conscience, and that will be a question of a social conscience embedded within secular society and in the church as a community. Now the church is encouraging citizens to take their part in building a new society, it will have to consider whether it cannot itself have a political programme and also provide some political training.The churches provided sanctuary under oppression and a starting point for critical movements, but they are not capable of being a permanent political platform. In a democracy on the Western model the church and state need to be separate, and political responsibility lies with the citizens. The church will have to see that Christians are able to bear this responsibility. That calls for training, as was recognized by the seventh special synod of bishops, on the role and mission of the laity in the world.

What is necessary in a post-Marxist and post-modern society, given increasing rationalization, is an ongoing concern for the human person, for the personal identity of men and women, which is determined by their own individual life-histories, their sex, upbringing, language, social context and belief. People make history and the future on the basis of this personal identity, and they may not hand it over to collectives, programmes and ideologies. All men and women bear the divine image within them.

Anton G. Weiler

For this special column I am indebted to articles in NRC Handelsblad, especially by P. Schnabel (23 December 1989), H. Smeets (6 January 1990), B. Knapen (6 February and 5 May 1990), J. van Doorn (8 February 1990), R. van den Boogaard (17 March 1990), G. Konrad (6 April 1990), M. Leyendekker (23 April 1990) and P. Michelsen (23 April 1990).

I · Theory: State of the Question

Vatican II and the Collegiality of Bishops

A Reading of *Lumen Gentium* 22 and 23

Herwi Rikhof

Introduction

In the search for the meaning of a text, the text itself must be primary; the text itself is of decisive importance in the definition of what is said, resolved, suggested, intended, kept silent about, or denied in the text. But in the framework of the search for the meaning of a text questions are also raised about the role which the intention of the writer has in the definition of meaning: is this of importance, can it provide clarification on some points, does this determine the meaning? And the same questions are raised in connection with preliminary drafts and sketches. Different answers have been given to these questions, as is evident, for example, from the discussion of the historical-critical method within exegesis. Without going into these questions in detail now, my starting point for the reading which follows is that intention and prehistory are not superfluous to a good understanding of the text, that they can offer help in explaining characteristics or peculiarities of the text, and so can contribute towards defining its significance.

If we look in the documents of Vatican II for texts in which the collegiality of bishops is discussed, two documents seem to be relevant: the Dogmatic Constitution on the Church, *Lumen Gentium* (1964), and the Decree on the Pastoral Office of the Bishops in the Church, *Christus Dominus* (1965). Of these two documents the former has the more important status. Moreover on the issue of collegiality there are no great differences between *Christus Dominus* and *Lumen Gentium*; *Lumen Gentium* is cited explicitly and with approval in *Christus Dominus*. Therefore in what follows we can concentrate on a reading of part of *Lumen Gentium*, paragraphs 22 and 23.

As I have already indicated, intention and prehistory are also involved in analysis aimed at a better understanding of this text. When it comes to intention, a number of practical problems arise. Who are the authors of the Constitution: the members of the commission which produced the various texts or the council fathers who discussed, accepted and subscribed to the texts? Given the theology of the council, the council fathers must be regarded as the authors. But in that case the following problem arises. Anyone who looks at the verbal and written interventions in the acts of the council will find it difficult to arrive at anything like *the* intention, given the large number of these interventions and the difference between them. Given the uniqueness of the council as an event, the intention seems to be limited to two actions: the rejection of the first draft during the first session and the publication of the *nota praevia* at the time of the final discussions.

Decisions also have to be made over the prehistory. If we take the history of the origin of *Lumen Gentium* in a broad sense, a large number of texts and studies are important. But if we take this history in a limited sense, namely up to the point of the preliminary drafts of the final text, then five texts are relevant. First there is the schema by G. Philips which circulated during the period of the first session. The second version of this was accepted as the starting point for their work by the commission charged with writing a new schema on 6 March 1963. That work resulted in a third version which was sent to the council fathers during summer 1963 and discussed during the second session. On the basis of this discussion the first version of a new schema was written in the period November 1963–April 1964: the second version contains in addition the amendments of Paul VI. This version was sent to the council fathers in July 1964. The final text of *Lumen Gentium* is the third version of this third schema.[1]

1. *Lumen Gentium* on the collegiality of bishops

Paragraphs 22 and 23, which deal with the collegiality of bishops, are in the third chapter of the Constitution, after three paragraphs which deal with the origin of the episcopate and before the paragraphs on the threefold task of the bishops and those on priests and deacons. This means that the theme of collegiality occupies a prominent place: what is held in common comes before the individual elements (task) or the distinguishing features (priests, deacons). This structure reflects the structure of *Lumen Gentium* as a whole. In other words, the constitution's view of the church generally, the characteristic of which is that what is held in common has priority over marks of differentiation, is expressed in reflection on the ministry. But the parallels with this view of the church and its influence go even further. In the Constitution, that which is held in common is set within a theological or salvation-historical approach to the church. This approach is called theological or salvation-historical because a link with the saving actions of God, Father, Son and Spirit, in history has a central place in it.

Characteristic of this approach is attention on the one hand to the 'inner dimension', to grace and salvation, and on the other to its historical manifestation. This new view, which may in fact claim to be the oldest and most important within the history of the church, can also be described as a view of *communio*. It is logical that when an important question is discussed within the framework of such a view, this view should make itself felt in the presentation and the argument. In other words, the salvation-historical framework determines which aspects are noted and given attention, and also what is accepted as an argument.

Now in the first paragraphs, the origin of the episcopate is described in terms both of its historical roots and of its sacramental character, and in this way the broad theological framework of the *communio* view is taken up. And this framework returns when there is express mention of the college of bishops: the first part of 22 is a repetition and summary of 19–21. The structure of the whole of *Lumen Gentium* and its far-reaching theological consequences thus define not only the point at which the episcopate is spoken of (after the people of God) but also what is said about the episcopate itself. In this way great weight is attached to collegiality and it is given an extra foundation: the collegiality of the bishops is not primarily (or, to put it less strongly, not just) a question of bishops or a view of the ministry, but primarily (or also) a question of the church or a view of the church. The collegiality of bishops belongs in a church as community, or, to put it even more strongly: the two cannot be separated.

The paragraph about the college of bishops and its head (22) can be divided into three sections: one on origins, one on power and the relationships of authority within the college, and one on the exercising of power by the college. In the section on origins, a connection is made between the college of bishops and the college of apostles, and a number of historical facts in the practice of the church are recalled, from which the existence and importance of collegiality emerges. The ecumenical councils are said to be the clearest evidence. Membership of the college is located in consecration and communion with the head and members of the college. In the section on authority it is said of both college and pope that they have supreme and complete power within the church. On relationships, it is ruled that the college has no authority without the pope, who can always exercise his power freely. In the last section it is stated that the college expresses both difference and unity and exercises its power in the ecumenical council, though other forms of collegial action are also possible.

The paragraph on relationships within the college (23) can also be divided into three sections. The first section deals with the link between the bishop and the local church, in which the bishop is the foundation of the unity of the local church and represents it: the one catholic church exists through and in the local churches, and the college of bishops with the pope represents the whole church. The second section discusses the care of all bishops, as members of the college, for the whole church, this care being extended both to those who are members of the church and to those who are not. In the third section attention is paid to the difference in traditions which has developed through history and to contemporary possibilities of collegiality. These three sections are connected with what has gone before by the observation that the solidarity of the college is also expressed in the mutual relationships of the bishops.

If we look at the paragraphs briefly and quite formally in this way, the first striking thing is the way in which themes and features emerge which are typically part of the salvation-historical view of *communio*. Apart from the repetition of the framework, to which I have already drawn attention, these are: the practice of the early church, which is used as an argument for the existence of the college of bishops; membership in terms of sacramental consecration, which refers back to what is said in the previous paragraph about the primarily sacramental character of the episcopal office; concern for the service which the college gives to the church community; the many forms in which this service has taken and can take shape; and the importance of the local church community.

If the paragraphs are looked at in this way, it is further striking that the organization and structuring of themes is somewhat untidy and, more importantly, is to some degree in tension with the framework which was sketched out earlier. Now the question of the competence of the pope and the college dominates the whole exposition, while it would be more in keeping with the expectations raised by the salvation-historical context for this question to be discussed after and in the framework of questions about unity and common concern. One could just as legitimately, indeed more legitimately, argue that the course of the exposition would have been served by a transposition of the second part of 22 with 23 and an integration of 23 into 22. In the exposition, then, after the comments on origins attention would first have been paid to the mutual relationships in the broadest sense of the term, and then to the function of the college within the church community, in which both the ecumenical council and the other forms emerge as the different ways by which this function is realized; finally attention would be paid to the specific role of the pope in the whole question.

The tension which emerges here can also be found in the introduction, in which the purpose of the chapter is indicated. The doctrine concerning bishops is to be interpreted in connection with Vatican I, and especially with what is said about the pope there. This point is important, because it brings out very sharply the question of the framework. Is the doctrine of Vatican I, which is characterized by an apologetic, legalistic and ahistorical view of the church, and is, moreover, focussed on the pope, now put within a collegial view of the office of bishop, which now belongs in a broad salvation-historical view of the church as *communio*? Or does the Vatican I view of the church remain the framework, some of the secondary features of which are now to be stressed differently and possibly even supplemented? The formula *in eodem incepto pergens* is used for the connection with Vatican I. This formula can be read in two ways.

It can be translated as 'going further in the same intent', and this is how G. Philips renders it.[2] In that case it indicates that the Vatican I teaching about the pope forms the framework for the doctrine of the episcopate. Here the tension becomes clear: from the beginning and as matter of course the college of bishops is a rival element. But the phrase can also be understood neutrally, as meaning 'following', 'after', 'supplementing', which is how Philips himself takes it in his commentary on the Constitution.[3] However, understood in this way this formula does not offer any solution. It even camouflages the problem, because the pressing question of the framework is concealed. So in both cases there are problems and unresolved tensions.

The same tension returns at the lowest level of the text, as it were within the sections, and then becomes even clearer. This can easily be seen in the part on the exercising of authority. The statement that the ecumenical council is the solemn way in which the college of bishops exercises full and supreme power over the whole church is directly followed by a remark about the role and above all the competence of the pope in such councils. The same procedure is followed in the other collegial acts. The tone is in both cases negative and limiting. Similar remarks are also made in the paragraph about the relationships within the college before the discussion of the dissemination of the faith. On the one hand it is stressed, with a reference to scripture and tradition, that the responsibility for dissemination lies with the whole college, but on the other hand it is said that this concern is entrusted to Peter in particular.[4]

The tension emerges most clearly in the part about the authority of the college of bishops. The course of the argument and the way in which it is put are revealing. This part begins with a sentence in which the use of 'however' (*autem*) suggests a contrast with what has gone before. In the preceding section the existence and importance of the college is indicated with reference to scripture and tradition. Moreover a negative phrase is used in the main sentence: the college has no authority (*auctoritatem non habet*). The subordinate clause which indicates the conditions on which authority is spoken of is dominated by 'the pope of Rome', who is said to be Peter's successor and head of the college; it is also said that this primacy over leaders and believers remains unassailed. In this first sentence it is also striking that the verbs of the main clause and the subordinate clause do not match: 'have authority' and 'understand'. In the subordinate clause one would expect a verb like 'function', or in the main clause a formula which has something to do with 'understanding' rather than 'have no authority'.

The next sentence is not about the college but about the pope, and its aim is to support the remarks in the subordinate clause of the first sentence: the connection is indicated with 'for' (*enim*). This sentence is dominated by absolutes, words which exclude a relationship or relativity: 'pastor of the whole church' (*totius Ecclesiae pastoris*), 'full, supreme and universal power' (*plenam, supremam et universalem potestatem*), 'always' (*semper*), 'freely' (*libere*). This character is further stressed by the definition of power 'by virtue of his charge' (*vi muneris sui*).

Then comes a sentence about the college as the subject of supreme and full power in the universal church. By means of 'however' (*autem*), the formula suggests a contrast with what has gone before, while 'also' (*quoque*) suggests a resemblance. The verb *exsistit* indicates that in contrast to the pope, here there is no question of a complete identification. This main clause is overloaded with subordinate statements and subordinate clauses. The framework of thought about the college as this is expounded in the first two paragraphs of this chapter and repeated in the first part of this paragraph is once again repeated through two subordinate clauses: 'is the successor to the college of the apostles in their role as teachers and pastors, and in it the apostolic college is perpetuated'. At the same time, a definition indicates the link with the pope and does so in an absolute way: 'one with . . . and never without' (*una cum . . . numquam sine*). This is stressed once again in a subordinate sentence, in which it is said that power can be exercised only (*nonnisi*) with the assent of the pope.

The final sentence of this part is an argument for this central sentence and contains scriptural references. Here the same structure returns that we already noticed in the previous sentences. The first concern is for Peter, and he is surrounded by absolute terms: 'only one' (*unum Simonem*), 'pastor of his (Christ's) whole flock' (*pastorem totius sui gregis*). In the second instance the college of apostles is spoken of and defined as 'bound up with its head' (*suo Capiti coniuncto*). In the subsequent mention of the college, the task of binding and loosing is first said to be given to Peter and afterwards 'also to the college'. The verbs which are used in connection with Peter express directness: 'appointed' (*posuit . . . constituit*), while a more distanced and indirect formula is used of the college: 'is clearly given' (*tributum esse constat*), a formula which might suggest contradiction and doubt.

So this reading discloses a text full of obscurities, contrary movements and unresolved tensions. Central to it is the framework within which the collegiality is expressed. Is this observation the last word, or can and must not more be said, if prehistory and intention are also involved in the reading?

2. History of origins

Anyone who looks at the successive versions of the preliminary drafts will be struck first of all by the fact that the first draft by Philips (November 1962) is not completely different from the official schema. There are important differences in themes and tone, but to some degree aim and text have also been taken over. One interesting and relevant example is the paragraph about the primacy and the episcopate, where collegiality is mentioned. If one looks at the overall plan of the chapter, it emerges that Philips has largely taken it over from the schema, but has filled it out, *inter alia* by opening paragraphs about the biblical roots of episcopacy and the college of bishops, and has extended it by adding paragraphs on the threefold ministry. This explains the striking place of the paragraphs about collegiality, which come only at the end of the chapter: a place which contrasts with the new concern for the college at the beginning of the chapter. Because he has added new paragraphs on the biblical foundation of the college of bishops specifically at the beginning of the schema, on the one hand the plan of the official schema has been changed, but on the other hand because he has kept the plan, the change has not been carried through or thought through consistently.

A few remarks need to be made about this method of adopting on the one hand and changing on the other. It is clear that as a result, from the beginning a tension between two different interests and views of the church has been built into the text. In other words, from the beginning the text is a compromise text with all the advantages and disadvantages of such a document. So it is evident why this text was accepted by the commission, and not one of the many other drafts which went the rounds. The suggestion of using the official schema as a basis, despite the criticism of the council fathers, was indeed rejected, but the radical alternative of a completely new beginning was evidently not possible. Hence it is also clear that if the relationships between these views or interests have not been properly clarified or regulated, there is a source of constant tension and unevenness here. It is significant that the formula which is used in the introduction to indicate the connection with Vatican I is the ambivalent *in eodem incepto pergens*, and that this formula is maintained right down to the final text.

Anyone who looks at the successive versions will also note that the developments, changes and supplements are such that the tension is not resolved but intensified. These developments take two directions. So in the second version (end 1962-beginning 1963) more attention is paid to collegiality: the paragraphs on collegiality are brought to the fore and instead of 'about primacy and episcopate' the words used are now 'the episcopal college and its head'. In the actual paragraph concern for the college is even intensified: there is no reference to scriptural support for the existence of the college, nor is there a reference to the old liturgical practice of the participation of several bishops in the consecration of bishops. Next to this a section is inserted, in which a definition of the college is given. The part about the college as subject of the supreme power, which in the previous version was still in the other paragraph about the relationship of the bishops to the universal church, is now incorporated into this paragraph. The actions of the college are also extended: there is mention not only of the ecumenical council but also of other possibilities (written consultation). In the paragraph about relationships between the bishops within the college the 'collegial sense' is a new element; that sense can take concrete form in the collaborative associations of bishops. So in this version there is a clear line which stresses the importance of the college; after a historical statement there is a definition of concept and function.

But in the third version (May 1963) a number of changes were made in the paragraph about the episcopal college and its head, as a result of which this clear structure becomes less clear. The changes, which are as follows, relate to the power and the role of the pope. In the definition, 'the college is not authentic unless understood . . .' is replaced by 'the college has no authority unless . . .'.[5] And the following part on its function (the subject of the supreme power) is prefaced by 'the pope of Rome has full and universal power in the church of himself (*per se*)'. More attention is also paid to the role of the pope in the part about the ecumenical council. In place of the observation that there can be no question of an ecumenical council unless the pope has approved or recognized it, which is almost just a reminder, the summoning of an ecumenical council is said to be the prerogative of the pope; in addition it is observed that from a historical perspective there can be no question of an ecumenical council unless it has been confirmed or recognized as such by the pope. Changes have also been made in the same direction in the part about the other forms of collegiality. To the collegial power there is now the addition 'one with the pope', and elements from the observations about ecumenical councils return: the pope invites a collegial action or freely approves it, so that it becomes an authentic collegial action. As a result of these changes the third version, more than the second, is characterized by power and the exercise of power, and above all more by competition and competence.

So at the moment when the council fathers got the new schema, the tension present in the first draft was heightened by developments in two directions. The tension became even greater when in the summer the decision was taken to preface the chapter about the hierarchy with a chapter about the people of God. In this way the communal aspect takes priority within the view of the church, although the far-reaching consequences of this have not yet been drawn.

We can see the same pattern of development in the subsequent phase. In the first version (April 1964), into which the discussions and suggestions for change by the council fathers were incorporated, intensifications of collegiality can be found at different points. Alongside the argument from liturgical praxis the historical basis for the existence of the college is now broadened by references to the communion between bishops and with the pope, which *inter alia* is expressed in the ecumenical councils. The ecumenical council is no longer characterized as an 'extraordinary and solemn' means of exercising power, but is now only called 'solemn', i.e. ordinary. One new feature is a part about the membership, in which not only is a legal argument given, but sacramental consecration is the first basis mentioned. In the paragraph about the relationships between bishops, in a new section the special character of the local church is stressed, with a reference to the differences between traditions and their riches.

But especially in the second version, into which the amendments of Paul VI have been worked, a number of changes can be noted in the part about the function or the power of the college, all of which are connected with the role of the pope and all of which strengthen this authority and contrast it with that of the college. Paramount here are the descriptions which on reading *Lumen Gentium* strike one as being absolutes: no attack on the power of the primacy, the pastor of the whole church, always free exercise of power, only to Simon.

The analysis of the development demonstrates that the tension and the contradictions which have been noted in the final text of *Lumen Gentium* have deep and strong roots. Although indications can be found in the developments (especially aim and structure, growth in concern and importance) that the theme of collegiality and the salvation-historical *communio* framework associated with it is determinative, this is not immediately clear. But it is clear that in the process the quite unambiguous formulations about collegiality are worked over in a way which increases the tension. Therefore it is also necessary to consider the intention of these considerations and to ask whether this was also deliberate.

3. The intention

3.1. The rejection of the first scheme

On 13 November 1962 the schema on the church, the result of two years' work, was presented to the council fathers. In the first week of December it was discussed. Cardinal Ottaviani presented it with a speech in which he said that the criticism which was slowly becoming familiar would also burst out here. The reception in fact ranged from being critical to being very critical. During the discussion it became increasingly clear that the majority did not want to accept the schema in principle and thought that it must be sent back for radical rewriting and a total revision.[6]

The schema that was rejected consisted of eleven chapters. After a first chapter on the nature of the striving church there were chapters on membership, the ministry, resident bishops, evangelical perfection, the laity, teaching authority, obedience, relations between church and state, and the ecumene. In the chapter on resident bishops the task of the bishop, the relationship between the pope and the episcopate and the relationship between the bishop and the whole church and the college of bishops were discussed.

From the structure and the titles of the chapters there already emerges a view of the church which is strongly interested in its legal and institutional aspects and which displays the characteristics of the apologetic approach which for centuries had dominated official thought about the church. In the first chapter this emerges from the total identification of the mystical body of Christ with the Roman Catholic Church. In the next chapters this church is looked at from above. The relationship within the church is expressed in terms of speaking (the ministry) and listening (the laity); relations with the outside world are expressed in terms of international relationships. In the chapter on resident bishops this view of the church is expressed in the permanent and almost exclusive concern for power and rules. Two matters are discussed in the paragraph about the college of bishops: power and the exercising of power, and membership. The college of bishops is said to be the subject of full and supreme power, though this power is legitimately exercised in an extraordinary way and in subjection to the representative of Christ. Before these statements a reference is made to the theology of the ecumenical councils on the basis of which it is said that the college 'is believed' (*creditur*) to be subject. The way of exercising power is called 'special' because – as emerges from a footnote – ecumenical councils are not necessary. With this is associated the conclusion that an action of the college, while legal, does not have a divine constitution. As for membership of the college, it is stated that all resident bishops who live in peace with the apostolic see are members by right (*suo iure*). No one can be a member without implicit or explicit assent to Peter's successor.

As I have said, this schema was sharply criticized. The most telling criticism came from the Bishop of Bruges, De Smedt, who dismissed the document as legalistic, triumphalistic and clerical. These three terms can be used as a negative indication of the intention of the council fathers. If one takes the whole text of *Lumen Gentium* and compares it with the first schema, one can see the positive alternatives from the structure and the themes. What comes first is not the legal aspect, nor the power structures, but the mystery of God, the bond with Father, Son and Spirit, the history of salvation and grace for men and women. The church is not primarily the hierarchy, nor is it characterized by a two-way traffic of speaking and listening. It is first of all the people of God, the community of believers who on the basis of their baptism participate in the priestly, kingly and prophetic tasks of Christ; within this community the ministry is a service to the community. The church itself does not have a central place nor is it the end, but it is transparent and points to God and the world; it is sacrament, in other words the instrument and sign of the unity of God with men and women. It is the beginning of the kingdom of God; it is on the way and in need of constant reformation.

Even if there were no alternatives, the negative start should be part of the interpretation of *Lumen Gentium*, but now that there clearly are alternatives, these must bear some weight in establishing the meaning of this document as a council document in cases of ambiguity or obscurity.[7] If we focus on the question of collegiality on this basis, it has to be said that the ambiguity and tension which emerge in the final text, the roots of which emerge in the preliminary history, can and must be solved in principle with a reference to this intention. The framework is not Vatican I but Vatican II.

3.2 *The* nota praevia

The so-called *nota praevia*, in which four points in the interpretation of *Lumen Gentium* 22 are defined, has been much discussed and assessed in extremely different ways. The text can be so interpreted that at certain points the note gives a clarification which is perhaps not superfluous, but still not really necessary, and at other points in fact says the same thing as *Lumen Gentium*. However, the text can also be read in such a way that, particularly over the position of the pope, it shows such differences from the Constitution as to restrict *Lumen Gentium*. It is important to discuss this briefly in connection with the intention.

The third and fourth points touch on the heart of the matter: the college as the subject of supreme and full power. Two distinctions are made: on the one hand between pope and college (pope and bishops) and on the other hand within the college between the pope as head and the bishops. In both cases the position of the pope is not discussed and there is inequality in the relationships. These two elements emerge in the different remarks which are made directly about the pope and in the one remark about the college. The pope is entrusted with the care of the whole flock, which he can exercise either personally or collegially, depending on his judgment (*iudicium*). If he exercises it collegially, he follows his own insight (*secundum propriam discretionem*) over the way in which this happens; he does this with a view to the wellbeing of the church. He exercises his power at all times as he wills (*ad placitum*), as his office requires. Of the college it is said only that while this exists at all times it is not permanently active as a college.

As I have said, this text can be read in two ways, and arguments for both of them can be found in the text. For the view that no great differences can be demonstrated between *Lumen Gentium* and the *nota*, reference can be made for the college to two points: the distinction 'is always present, but not permanently active' makes its existence clear; the statement that the college can act only with the compliance of the pope indicates that there is no question of its being dependent on an external authority. Moreover, it can be argued that in *Lumen Gentium* and the *nota* the pope is concerned for the whole flock, that he acts freely by virtue of his office, and that he is the head of the college, which cannot function without him. Finally, reference can be made to the definitions in connection with the church's exercise of power (the wellbeing of the church, the requirements of the office) which put the strictly legal aspect in a wider and more important framework of morality and which imply obedience to e.g. revelation.

The view that there are great differences can be supported by reference to the way in which the pope is the main object of attention. The framework for the thought about collegiality is formed by Vatican I. Moreover the independence of the pope is expressed not so much in absolute as in absolutist terms: according to his judgment, according to his own insights, as he pleases. The following point can also be made in this connection. In one of the last revisions the commission decided not to accept a proposal for change from Paul VI because it was superfluous and too simplistic. This was the formula: the pope, completely united with the one Lord (*uni domino devictus*), calls on the bishops for collegial action. The *nota* not only reverses this decision; it expresses a stronger claim. Finally, it can be noted that collegiality is not only limited by this absolutism but is also undermined by the emphasis that the college does not act permanently. Collegiality is seen only in a particular, special form and thus belongs more to the first schema than to the last. And the undermining goes still further, since it is argued that the college has authority because failure to recognize it would also be to fail to recognize the authority of the pope, who is the head of the college. The reference to the independence of the bishop and the local church has thus disappeared completely.[8]

At this point it seems important to consider not only the *nota* but also its circumstances: in other words, not only the text but also the fact of the *nota*. At the beginning of the *nota* it is made clear that the commission is its author. Although it is clear that the commission did not take the initiative for the *nota* and did not work alone in preparing it, that does not alter the fact that the *nota* is and remains only something from the commission.[9]

If full weight is attached to this fact, the interpretation of the *nota* as being in agreement with *Lumen Gentium* (and thus superfluous) is the most logical one. The importance of the *nota* then seems to be more its psychological effect than its content. It played a role in the establishment of a consensus, but does not contribute to any insight in terms of content into this consensus. It is like a ladder which can be removed because its purpose has been achieved. Even if this logical solution is not chosen, the *nota* is and remains something from the commission and not an indication of the intention of the council fathers.

But there is yet another side to the *nota*. It is introduced with the information that it comes 'from a higher hand' and it is not signed by the president of the commission but by the Secretary General of the council. Moreover, the note is presented as the normative interpretation of *Lumen Gentium* and added to the council documents as part of them. When the *nota* was read out to the council fathers on 16 November, one day before the last separate vote on chapter 3, it was the first time that they had heard of it. The *nota* had been prepared in secret and did not come into being at the request of the council fathers. Nor could there be discussion of the note or a vote on it. All in all this was an extraordinary procedure. These facts point strongly in the direction of an interpretation of the note in terms of differences from the text of *Lumen Gentium*, which had already been accepted earlier with a two-thirds majority. For why should this extraordinary step have been taken if the content of the note agrees with *Lumen Gentium*? And this procedure seems somewhat heavy-handed for just a psychological influence on a general vote. If the *nota* needs to be interpreted in this way, it seems paradoxically enough to be in fact an indication of the intention of the council fathers: it indicates what they did not want. The limiting, centralist interpretation of collegiality as it emerges in the *nota* goes against the overwhelming majority and must be looked at in these terms. The second important element which is important for the intention thus leads to the same conclusion as the first.

Conclusion

It emerges from a reading of *Lumen Gentium* 22–23 that the text does not give a clear and unambiguous view of the place and content of collegiality. It emerges from the analysis of the prehistory that the tension was always there and has deep roots. From an analysis of the intention it emerges that in principle the opposed movements need to be resolved in the direction of a view in which the central place of collegiality is given full weight. It must emerge from history subsequent to the council whether this solution in principle has also become a reality.

Translated by John Bowden

Notes

1. For the various texts see G. Alberigo and F. Magistretti (eds.), *Constitutionis Dogmaticae Lumen Gentium Synopsis Historica*, Bologna 1975.
2. An English translation can be found in *Vatican Council II, The Conciliar and Post-Conciliar Documents*, ed. Austin Flannery OP (1981).
3. *L'Église et son mystère au IIe concile du Vatican. Histoire, texte et commentaire de la Constitution Lumen Gentium*, Paris 1967.
4. Reference is made in a footnote to the encyclical *Grande munus* of Leo XII, but the formulation is in fact a literal translation from Pius XI's encyclical *Rerum Ecclesiae*.
5. This is the explanation of the strange combination of 'have authority' and 'understand' referred to above. This change of 'is authentic' into 'has authority', resulting in a forced combination, is perhaps the most telling and characteristic example of what constantly took place in the preparation.
6. To mention some council fathers who argued for a radical revision of the schema (the numbers indicate the page in the *Acta Synodalia Sacrosancti Concilii Oecumenici Vaticani Secundi*, Rome (1963, I): Alfrink (136), De Smedt (142–4), Döpfner (185–6), Marty (193), Huyghe (197), Frings (in the name of all the German-speaking bishops) (220), Suenens (222–7), Bea (230), Montini (291–4), Ghattas (377), Volk (388).
7. One can of course argue that the view as a whole or in parts is not true, but one cannot argue that this view is not the view of the council.
8. For an extended analysis of the *nota* and a detailed argument especially in favour of the second view see J. Ratzinger, 'De bischoppelijke collegialiteit. Een theologische beschouwing', in G. Barauna (ed.), *De Kerk van Vaticanum II*, Deel II, Bilthoven 1966, 46–71, esp. 62–8, and his commentary in *Das Zweite Vatikanische Konzil (LThK)*, I, 1966, 348–59.
9. See Ratzinger, 'De bischoppelijke collegialiteit' (n.8), 62f.

The Collegiality of the Synod of Bishops: An Unresolved Problem

Jan Grootaers

At first sight it might have seemed quite easy to give a rapid survey of what each of the extraordinary synods of 1969 and 1985 understood by collegiality. In addition, it would have been necessary to see the conclusions which each of these two assemblies drew from it. In reality, this has proved much more complicated than appeared at first sight and at all events is too complex to be undertaken within the space of a review article.

So my intention is to sketch out a brief comparison between the two synods by way of introduction and then to analyse at greater length the 1985 debate and some of its conclusions.

I. Introductory comparison

On first impressions it is difficult to imagine two more contrasting events in the church than the synods of 1969 and 1985: the general atmosphere and historical context were profoundly different, and the theological environment and 'collective memory' were not the same. The majority of the fathers in the 1985 synod were almost completely ignorant of the conclusions of the 1969 synod, and those who directed the 1985 synod were not concerned to recall the precedents of 1969.

Nevertheless there were also links between the two synods. Both were 'extraordinary' (thus bringing together only the presidents of episcopal conferences) and both were devoted to an evaluation of the reception of Vatican II, for the most part to the theme of collegiality.

A distinction needs to be made here between the official agenda, which was concerned entirely (in 1969) or partly (in 1985) with the question of 'collegiality in the church', and what in fact became the central preoccupations. The main preoccupations of the 1969 synod were on the one hand how to specify the limits of the function of the primate and on the other hand how to establish a certain reciprocity between episcopates and the Holy See.

The question of the limits of the function of the primate had already played a considerable role at Vatican II. In May 1964 Paul VI had sent the doctrinal commission of the council an amendment according to which the pope, in calling on the college, 'is accountable only to God' (*uni Domino devinctus*). This proposal was rejected because it was too simplistic: conciliar theologians like Mgr G. Philips and Fr J. Ratzinger were explicit in this respect.[1] The introductory *relatio* of the 1969 synod (by Cardinal F. Marty) foresaw 'objective norms' to which the exercise of the primatial ministry remained subject: this idea was taken up in the final report of the synod (by Fr A. Anton).

As for reciprocity between the 'centre' and the 'periphery', the fathers of the 1969 synod were almost unanimous in calling for the implementation of co-operation and co-ordination (specifically by the regular exchange of information) between the Holy See and the episcopal conferences. The role of the latter would thus be singularly increased. Moreover the 1969 fathers, above all in their *circuli minores*, wanted to develop the synod itself in order to 'strike out on a new course in the collegial work of bishops'.

Unfortunately none of these explicit wishes finally made their way to the *vota* of the 1969 synod, the official version of which was considerably watered down at the last minute.

In 1985, other preoccupations in fact ended up by dominating the synod debate: there we see a concern (which is sometimes implicit) to stress the continuity of Vatican II with previous councils and with the recent tradition of the church. The obvious aim of this was to reassure troubled spirits. There was also a preoccupation with stressing the spiritual dimensions of ecclesiology while at the same time relativizing the necessary reform of ecclesial structures.

This difference between two synods of bishops, both of which dealt with collegiality, reveals to what extent even the dynamic of the synod changed between 1969 and 1985. One thing seems certain: the questions raised in 1969 by the majority of the fathers about the structures of the church were not answered at that time; these same questions resurfaced at the 1985 synod. It cannot be denied that in this respect at least one firm bond linked the two assemblies.

As proof of this one need only refer to the end of this paragraph on ecclesiology in the introductory report by Cardinal Danneels in November 1985: 'Theological questions remain to be resolved: what is the relationship between the universal church and particular churches? How is collegiality to be promoted? . . . Moreover the respondents mention their desire to see a marked improvement in relationships between the particular churches and the Roman Curia. Finally, the reports stress the need for information, mutual consultation and intensified communication.'[2] These few lines from 1969 faithfully but unintentionally sum up the agenda of the 1985 synod!

II. The 1985 debate in plenary session

It is difficult to underestimate the importance of the surveys that were undertaken in preparation for the 1985 synod. For the conferences of bishops it was no less than an evaluation of twenty years of the 'reception' of Vatican II. (It is regrettable that only a small part of this unique documentation has been published.)

Introductory report

The 'introductory report' by Cardinal G. Danneels, the official *relator* of the 1985 synod, seconded by Fr W. Kasper, the special secretary, is mainly based on the results of this preparatory survey. This report stresses the welcome and the positive results of Vatican II, despite the negative phenomena, which were not passed over in silence but treated with moderation. Thus from the start a tone was given to the synod, one which clearly contrasted with the unilateral interpretation given by Cardinal J. Ratzinger after the council in his interview 'This is why the faith is in crisis'.[3]

The author of the report tried to play down the existing tensions and also sought to forestall excessive polemic as far as possible. In the published agenda we can find the 'architecture of the work of the council':

1. The mystery of the church (*Lumen Gentium*)
2. The sources (Bible and liturgy)
3. The church as 'communion'
4. Mission today (*Gaudium et Spes*)

This same framework can be found in the intermediate report and the final report.

Ecclesiology is given a dominant place in this whole. If the period after the council gave rise to a renewed awareness of the prophetic mission and the responsibility of all the faithful, it nevertheless remains the case that the heart of the crisis is to be found in the doctrine of the church: this was received in a unilateral and superficial way. Hence also the crisis of confidence in the church. Thus the report which introduced the synod.[4]

However, the main concern of the bishops who were questioned was to promote a deeper understanding of the conciliar texts in order to arrive at an authentic implementation of them. After the euphoria following Vatican II and after the disappointment which ensued, a third phase began: that of a more balanced rediscovery of the texts of Vatican II.

The debate in plenary session is beyond doubt the most dynamic part of synodical procedure. In 1985 this debate allowed the great majority of the members of the synod to express their attachment to the great advances of Vatican II and their desire to add greater weight to specific applications. The current of faith and hope which then ran through the assembly raised great hopes for the coming 'reception' of the council texts. Those involved were far from being *laudatores temporis acti*.

Principal themes

Collegiality in the church, the theme of this article, was the main object of interventions by the representatives of the Western churches. In the eyes of the spokesmen of the young churches inculturation was the most urgent problem, with its applications to the liturgy, catchesis and also theological reflection.

Moreover one could note an interaction between the two subjects: the viability of inculturation in a particular area is essentially determined by the space for it which can be provided by the local church and the conference of bishops. We might say that the preoccupation of the young churches with being able to deploy the local church issued in the wider current of a collegial image of the church. The consequence of this characteristic 'detour' was that the interventions of the orators of the young churches were conceived in a more constructive manner, while certain spokesmen of the North Atlantic world sometimes displayed a more critical style towards the Roman authorities.

Besides, it was difficult always to make a very clear distinction between the question of conferences of bishops and that of collegiality. The synod fathers who spoke in favour of conferences of bishops or the synod of bishops either explicitly or implicitly took a position against a centralization inspired by Rome.

On the other hand one could note that the speeches which favoured centralization were critical of the role of the episcopal college and of certain areas in which the principle of collegiality applied. One of the crucial points of the debate on collegiality in November 1985 was certainly the question of the status of conferences of bishops. The negative positions of Cardinal Ratzinger in this respect aroused even the most pacific. A minority of fathers defended a restrictive reading of *Lumen Gentium*; they recognized the exercise of a true episcopal *magisterium* only in two instances: that of a general council and that of the individual bishop in his diocese. This minority trend called for an examination of the theological status of conferences of bishops and the breadth of their participation in the *magisterium* of the church in so far as such authority really existed.

However, a very large majority proved to defend a quite different vision of things. On the prompting of North American and Anglo-Saxon bishops a large number of fathers asked that the status of episcopal conferences should be based not only on motives of a pragmatic or legal kind but also on theological foundations. In this perspective it was implicitly recognized that the individual bishop had to take account of the authority of the conference and that the conference was authorized, having regard for the particular circumstances of its pastoral activities, to develop certain public standpoints, as for example in the United States. During the last decades we have in fact seen a wide diversification and an extraordinary vitality in the ordinary *magisterium* of the local churches: the standpoints of 'the Church' have thus come considerably closer to the concrete reality of the local church. This diversification in the area of social directives has been possible thanks to these applications of the principle of collegiality in the synods of bishops, continental conferences and national episcopates.

The centralizing tendency which had made itself felt in the final text of the *vota* of October 1969 was expressed with even more vigour by the minority trend of November 1985. If one day it were to end up as a fact it would constitute a grave threat to this whole fruitful development after the council. For the moment it should be noted that the final report of 1985 asked for a 'study' of the problem of the theological status of episcopal conferences *without any reference* either to the development called for by a large majority or to the restrictive interpretation desired by the minority trend.

Here we come upon a phenomenon which is very characteristic of this playing down of the problem of which the redactors of the conclusions of the 1985 Synod have been accused.

Argument

In a few words, what is now the current argument in favour of collegiality? The following statements were made to the plenary synod. It is with a view to more effective evangelization that the synod is urged to rest on the *affectus collegialis* of *Lumen Gentium* (no. 23) which tends to reinforce collegiality and to guarantee the doctrinal authority of the conferences of bishops (Malone, USA). It is necessary to seek a better balance between central power and local power in order to assure plurality in unity (Williams, New Zealand). While Vatican II had contributed to restoring the experience of the local church and developing its identity, a regrettable return to centralization could be noted. By contrast, the Roman Curia should encourage the local churches to develop their own responsibilities (Gran, Scandinavia; Winning, Scotland; S. E. Carter, Jamaica; F. X. Hadisumarta, Indonesia; Berg, Austria).

Better accord and wider consultation were needed between the local churches and the Roman Curia (Kitbunchu, Thailand). Numerous bishops also stressed that the competence and function, and also the secretariat, of the synod should be strengthened (Hermaniuk, Canada; Schwéry, Switzerland; Marty, France; McGrath, Panama).

The trend in favour of centralization was more articulate than in 1969 and moreover enjoyed the support of the curial authorities, even if numerically it remained in the minority. The *extensive* activity of the post-conciliar church had to give place to a more *intensive* activity: in this respect it was up to the synod to enlighten the church not just *qua* organization (with a distribution of powers) but above all as mystery (Meissner, East Berlin; Ratzinger, Curia).[5] To respond to the threat of the centrifugal forces in the church after Vatican II there was a need to reinforce central authority in the church (Höffner, Cologne; Lustiger, France; Araujo Sales, Brazil).

Between these two positions must be put the trend in favour of *inculturation* in which representatives of the young churches tended to a new conception of collegiality, centred on the solidarity and brotherhood between local churches (A. T. Sanon, Burkina Faso; F. Makouaka, Gabon; Kitbunchu, Thailand; Mayala, Tanzania).[6]

III. The concluding report

Observers have noted the radical change in tone which came about in the 1985 synod, from the phase of the *circuli minores* onwards. The intermediary report by Cardinal Danneels aimed at introducing changes in the *circuli minores* had already stressed what remained to be done: the agenda of the *circuli* tends to make these adopt a more negative perspective than that of the first week. Finally, it has to be noted that the final report no longer has the coherence of the introductory report, a quality due mainly to the inspiration of Fr W. Kasper. The final report no longer reflects all the exchanges in the synod.[7]

In the structure of the final report there is a need to distinguish between the explanatory paragraphs (27 in all) and the paragraphs of 'suggestions' (6 in all). The latter conclude the former. The fathers voted only on the 'suggestions'.

In a consideration of the chapter devoted to the church as *communion*, in which there is a discussion of collegiality, we can note some explanatory paragraphs which are of considerable interest and which then end up in some quite insignificant 'suggestions'. In particular churches in which one and the same eucharist is celebrated, the one universal church is truly present, 'so that the one and unique Catholic church exists in and through the particular churches' (*Lumen Gentium* 23), the principle of pluriformity in unity.[8]

The passage on collegiality (II C 4) recognizes that 'the ecclesiology of communion provides the sacramental foundation for collegiality. As a result of this, the theology of collegiality is far wider than its simple legal aspect.' Subsequently, however, a radical distinction is introduced between collegiality in the strict sense on the one hand, the most evident expression of which is in the ecumenical council, and various partial and indirect realizations in ecclesiastical law on the other. Among the latter the text gives a strange list which includes the synod of bishops, the conferences of bishops, the Roman Curia[9] and *ad limina* visits. One can find the main elements of this paragraph II C 4 of the synod report in the too little known address which Cardinal Hamer gave at the plenary meeting of the College of Cardinals held on the eve of the 1985 Synod.[10]

We then see that the collegial spirit has a concrete application in the conferences of bishops (II C 5). However, both these paragraphs end with a reservation: both collegiality and the conferences of bishops are at the service (*a*) of the college with the pope, (*b*) of individual bishops whose responsibility is inalienable. This double reservation explicitly limits in height and depth the area of freedom and competence which the conferences of bishops have at their disposal.

The following passage seems to me to be more positive and tending towards renewal: it is devoted to 'participation and co-responsibility in the church' (II C 6). This time the subject is relations of communion within the local church: between the bishop and his presbytery, between the laity and the clergy (including collaboration with women), and also within the new ecclesial base communities, 'which are thus a reason for great hope for the life of the church'.[11] So here we find the very principle of this synodicalism, without which the principle of collegiality remains in suspense.

As for the three final 'suggestions', the whole point of the synod debate is passed over in silence. The suggestions content themselves with three wishes: 1. the desire that Eastern codification be achieved as quickly as possible; 2. the wish for a study of the theological 'status' and the doctrinal authority of conferences of bishops, taking into account *Christus Dominus* no. 38 and canons 447 and 753 of the code (this last specification has been added to the text of the report by an unidentified hand); 3. a study is recommended of whether the principle of subsidiarity can be applied to the life of the church.[12]

In the intermediate report presented by Cardinal Danneels on the eve of the *circuli minores*, traces could still be found of the tensions which had been indicated in the course of the debate in plenary session and which the synod had been called to clarify: there was talk there of 'the collegiality which many fathers want to see made deeper and put into practice in a more effective way.'[13] But in the final suggestions the implementations desired by the majority of synod fathers have disappeared, while a questioning of the doctrinal authority of the conferences has been introduced.

Whereas in 1969, even in the weakened *vota*, it was still envisaged that the desired study on the doctrine of collegiality would be referred to the new International Theological Commission (and numerous fathers at that time wanted to reserve the right to see this work), the 1985 synod did not specify either the authority responsible for the study or any procedure allowing a degree of control. According to the well-known funnel effect it might be feared that the final report would be a regression from the synod, but the reality was worse: all the differing currents of opinion which emerged and even the emphasis of the previous paragraphs of the concluding report had disappeared.

IV. The main lacunae in the 1985 Synod

The main fault of the final report of December 1985 is its wish to relativize the importance of the structures of the church and the distribution of powers, in contrast to the introductory report, which still recognized the weight of these questions.

As I suspected in analysing the concept of 'communion' during the course of the synodical debates of 1969, this rich idea was reorientated in a very particular direction in the final document of 1985. There we read:

'consequently the ecclesiology of communion cannot be reduced merely to questions of organization or to problems which are simply related to power' (II C 1).[14]

In this way the final report, in an arbitrary fashion, imputes to the supporters of the actual practice of collegiality intentions which they do not have, and at the same time it can relativize the legitimate question of structures. In the chapter on the church as mystery we had already read: 'We cannot replace a false unilateral vision of the church as purely hierarchical with a new sociological conception which is equally unilateral' (II A 3).[15] In thus posing false dilemmas there is a failure to recognize the twofold character of the church, a reality which is both divine and human, both mystical and social.

'Others, yielding to the temptation to absorb all the human aspects of the church in the majesty of its supernatural origin, end up . . . evacuating the mystery by destroying its earthly reality.'[16] That is how Mgr Philips already put us on guard against any ecclesiological monophysitism!

Other important themes which had been stressed in the synodal *aula*, like the significance of the synod itself, and inculturation, are virtually absent from the concluding report. But the point where this best shows up its selective reading of the ecclesiology of Vatican II is certainly in the virtual disappearance of the church as people of God.

The overall evaluation of the 1985 synod depended largely on expectations. Some months before the opening of this synod, a large number of people were saying that the assembly would only serve to impose on the whole church the pessimistic reading of the post-conciliar period defended by Cardinal Ratzinger. We have seen that the initial report of the Danneels–Kasper team and an almost unanimous majority of bishops at first rejected such an interpretation.

However, some representatives of the local churches had hoped that the 1985 Synod would be the occasion for developing a response to the urgent pastoral challenges with which they found themselves confronted. But the formulation of the concluding report was so restricting that these expectations were also disappointed.

So at the end of the day we find a compromise which at first sight is an illusion – the synod ended in general euphoria – but which subsequently left an impression of disappointment and a bitter taste with both sides.

V. In conclusion: an experience of collegiality put into practice

The conception of collegiality at the extraordinary synod of 1969 still offered the riches of conciliar discussion but also perpetuated the climate of indecision of Vatican II. In 1969 the majority of fathers had not yet truly realized the whole significance of the *nota praevia*; they did not yet take into account the intensive use (and in their view abuse) which would be made of it.[17] The 1969 majority sought principally, if not exclusively, to arrive at practical ways of putting collegiality into practice, even if this was at the expense of any deeper doctrinal positions. Finally, this majority did not obtain either the forms it explicitly wanted or the doctrine which it voluntarily passed over in silence.

At the 1985 extraordinary synod the majority of the fathers were on the defensive: it was more a matter of preserving than of conquering. The general context was evidently very different. Cardinal Seper and Mgr Moeller were no longer directing the Doctrine of the Faith as in 1969, and the ruling authorities sought to 'frame' the post-conciliar dynamic, stressing more the phenomena of crisis. Finally in 1985 the conferences of bishops themselves, which in 1969 were considered standard-bearers for the future, were seeking to safeguard their own functioning.

The route followed between 1969 and 1985 can also be measured by the address, already quoted here, given by Cardinal J. Hamer, on 'The Ecclesiological Significance of the Roman Curia'. In it one can read that those who direct the Roman court 'are *like* the mediators of collegial feeling between the head and the members of the college. Often they have meetings *in the form of* a small permanent synod . . .' (my italics). Whereas the final document of 1985, edited in the circumstances with which we are familiar, seeks to 'individualize' the members of the episcopal college, a head of a court who is one of the most authoritative of figures seeks in turn to 'collegialize' the directors of the services of the Roman Curia. Here we really are at the opposite extreme to the requests of the majority of the synod fathers in 1969.

It can be noted that the majority of writers from the 'collegial' trend refer to the notion of communion which proved important at Vatican II when it was decided to insert the 'People of God' as a second chapter of *De Ecclesia*. The term refers to an idea common during the first millennium which denoted a reality that was both visible and invisible, that belonged to the world of the mysteries of faith. According to Dom O. Rousseau the idea of communion above all signifies *koinonia*, a circulation of the same spiritual goods between Christian brothers and sisters. If the term collegiality is to be applied by extension to the common priesthood of the faithful, then it will in fact be inadequate, because according to Vatican II it is limited to the *ordo episcoporum* as a principle of apostolicity. The notion of communion is then considered more appropriate to denote this vocation which is common to all.[18]

At the 1969 synod we saw quite a paradoxical use of the concept of communion. This very rich notion is orientated in a hierarchical direction which does not correspond to its original meaning, but is much wider. At the 1985 synod we again find this same particular orientation of communion in the final document, but this time going so far as to mute the 'people of God'![19]

If the extraordinary synods of 1969 and 1985 had had as their sole aim the function of resolving the implementation of collegiality in accordance with the texts of Vatican II, our survey would certainly be negative. However, these two episcopal assemblies were significant events because of the function of critical evaluation and collegial dialogue on the facts that they achieved.

The 1969 synod made possible a first awareness of the value of Vatican II after the council had been tested by the realities of the local church. The 1985 synod was an eloquent manifestation of the beneficial results of the council, and as a very clear expression of the will to pursue its reception is an important stage in the development of the church after the council.

Even if the request for the recognition of the deliberative competence of the synod of bishops, made in 1969 and repeated in 1985, has not been heard, the synodical assembly nevertheless remains a unique experience of collegiality put into practice. In this form the institution of the synod has an important value for the future, even if the texts which emerge from it are usually disappointing because they are never on the same level as the plenary sessions.

It seems to me necessary to stress in this way the possibility of experiencing collegiality in the Catholic church partially and provisionally, while waiting for its significance to be recognized fully and in ecclesial structures. It seems to me that it is only within this dynamic perspective that it remains possible to further the reception of the great project of Vatican II and to do so in the concrete reality of the life of the church.

Translated by John Bowden

Notes

1. Cf. G. Philips, *L'Église et son mystère au IIe Concile du Vatican*, Vol. 1, Paris 1967, 304; J. Ratzinger, 'Bekanntmachungen', *Lexikon für Theologie und Kirche – Das*

Zweite Vatikanische Konzil, Freiburg 1966, 1, 355f.; for the dossier on the amendment by Paul VI in May 1964 see J. Grootaers, *Primauté et Collégialité – Le dossier de G. Philips sur la Nota Explicativa Praevia*, Louvain 1986, 134–8.

2. Cf. *Vingt ans après Vatican II*, Paris 1986, 52f.

3. Cf. *Jesus*, November 1984.

4. The report by Cardinal G. Danneels is in *Vingt ans après Vatican II* (n. 3), 50, 52.

5. One can also read in the final report (II C 1): 'ecclesiology cannot be reduced purely to questions of organizations or problems which only concern simple powers.' See *Documentations Catholiques* 1909, 39. On numerous occasions Cardinal Ratzinger declared that it was unfitting to stress the question of powers in the church: a paradoxical opinion when one has powers of government and a preponderance of power in the present church!

6. In the 1969 synod a similar argument was developed by a number of bishops, including the Archbishop of Cracow, Cardinal K. Vojtyla.

7. J. Komonchak, 'The Theological Debate', *Concilium* 188, 1986, 62.

8. There is a synthesis of the work of the synod in *Documentations Catholiques* 1909, of 5 January 1986, 40.

9. See my remarks on the subject of the 'ecclesiological significance' of the Roman Curia at the end of the present article.

10. Cf. *Synode Extraordinaire*, Paris 1986, 598–602: at the start Cardinal J. Hamer made a 'capital distinction' between *collegial action*, which is reserved for the college as such, the head of which is the pope, and *collegial feeling*, an 'opportune expression' of which is the conference of bishops which comes under ecclesiastical law, with the aim of helping bishops who govern particular churches *iure divino*.

11. The text of the report is in *Documentations Catholiques* 1909, 40f.

12. The text of the report is in *Documentations Catholiques* 1909, 41.

13. *Relatio post disceptationem* of 29 November 1985, typescript document.

14. The schema preparing for the 1969 synod seeks to base its doctrine on the 'communion' in the church with its internal element (the spiritual goods in which the faithful participate) and its external element (which is proper to the social structure of the church). This communion is first applied to the faithful and then to the bishops. But as soon as this latter aspect is touched on, one feels that the notion is directed towards visible communion, with a hypertrophy of the local church of Rome, and there is a tendency to lapse into pre-conciliar categories. See Dom Olivier Rousseau, 'Le deuxième synode des évêques: collégialité et communion', *Irénikon* 42, 1969, 467–71.

15. The text of the report is in *Documentations Catholiques* 1909, 38.

16. Philips, *Église* (n. 1), 117f.; the concluding report seeks to relativize the importance of the debates on the structure in the church in a different way by appealing to the collegial spirit and its sacramental foundation, 'when it could as justly be argued that the questions arise precisely because the sacramental and collegial foundations require more appropriate structures and relationships': that is the opinion of Komonchak, 'Theological Debate' (n. 7), 57; see also U. Ruh, 'Konzilsbilanz nach 20 Jahren', *Herder Korrespondenz*, January 1986, 38, who has the same opinion.

17. A Acerbi, 'L'ecclésiologie à la base des institutions post-conciliaires', in *Les Églises après Vatican II*, ed. G. Alberigo, Paris 1981, 226.

18. Rousseau, 'Le deuxième synode' (n.14).

19. It would also be instructive to compare the development and application of this particular version of 'communion' at the two significant events which opened the present pontificate, i.e. the CELAM assembly at Puebla in 1979 and the special Synod of Dutch Bishops at Rome in 1980. The selective re-reading of Medellin at Puebla, eleven years after 1968, and the selective re-reading of Vatican II at the synod of 1985, twenty years after 1965, are based on a common vocabulary. This is a remarkable, but little-remarked, fact.

An Overview of Theologians' Positions: A Review of Major Writings and the State of the Question Today

Donato Valentini

This study deals with the problems and proposals in theological literature relating to episcopal collegiality after the council. It will not proceed strictly by historical and theological categories, analysing the thought of individual authors one by one, but rather logically and systematically on a thematic basis; where necessary, it will seek to relate authors' contributions critically to this basis.

1. Examples of methodology

If the formal relationship between the pope and the episcopal college is a matter of 'grappling with problems',[1] all the more so is episcopal collegiality overall. In seeking a solution to the problems it is important to pay attention to some examples of methodology.

First of all, in the case of episcopal collegiality there is a need to avoid purely deductive processes. Thus it would be wrong to say: the apostles formed a college, the bishops 'succeeded' the apostles, therefore the bishops form a college. To produce a correct historical and theological argument it is necessary to refer both to the college of the apostles and to the hierarchical, normative structure of the primitive church. As J. Ratzinger notes, it is not possible to give any theological foundation to the reality of the church without resorting to its life.[2] Moreover a return to history and historicity help to clarify some problems of episcopal collegiality. It is enough to recall here the complaints of the twelfth-century 'mendicants' and the development of private confession, the ideology of the sacramentality of the cardinalate and the reinterpretation of the category of *ius divinum*, because they are of at least indirect importance for our subject.

Secondly, in a reflection on episcopal collegiality it is necessary to maintain the well-known distinction between doctrine of faith and theology. This distinction allows us to overcome the difficulty posed by the fact that every now and then the *magisterium* 'abandons' positions which it had held previously. Thus Pius XII in the encyclicals *Mystici Corporis* (9 June 1943), *Ad Synarum gentes* (7 October 1955) and *Ad Apostolorum principis* (29 June 1958) taught that the power of episcopal jurisdiction, or of teaching and government, derives directly from the pope. However, Vatican II, for example in *Lumen Gentium* III.25, affirms that such power is conferred directly on the bishop by God through the sacrament of ordination. This is a view which I also hold. The position of Vatican II is theologically possible because and to the degree that the position of Pius XII does not constitute a doctrine of faith.

The third example of methodology concerns the relationship between the juridical and the theological interpretations of episcopal collegiality. Certainly, the social dimension is also a constitutive aspect of the mystery of the church. It is the basis for the legitimacy and need for a juridical approach to the church. However, that does not amount to authorizing cognitive processes aimed at autarchy. In a correct vision of the church the juridical is at the service of the 'theological' and needs to be integrated into it. The one comprises the other.[3] It follows that readings of episcopal collegiality which move unilaterally in the juridical sphere are destined to arrive at partial conclusions. This comment leads into the more general, and in part different, problem of the relationship between theological science and the 'humane sciences'; these enter into the theology of episcopal collegiality in a proper multidisciplinary and interdisciplinary perspective on the subject. One instance of this is the category of subsidiarity.[4]

The fourth and last example of methodology involves the logical approach to a treatment of collegiality which also seeks to be along the lines of a present-day perspective. Furthermore, it is not easy to respond to such demands, putting the various elements of discourse in a harmonious synthesis. It seems to me that in the period after the council it is increasingly possible to note a movement of thought which begins from the 'ecclesiology of communion', moves on to the sacramental foundation of collegiality', tries to delineate communion and law in the episcopal college, is involved in reflection about the subject or subjects of supreme power in the church, and finally discusses the forms of collegiality.

2. The priority of the 'ecclesiology of communion'

What remains in my mind at the end of an investigation of episcopal collegiality in theology since Vatican II is first of all the conviction of the priority, in terms both of truth and of logical organization, of the 'ecclesiology of communion'. It is not possible within the space of this article to give a detailed analysis of its emergence in the sphere of episcopal collegiality. However, it does seem relevant and useful to offer a brief survey which stresses the criteria of the system and the synthesis on both a chronological and an analytical level. By the nature of things, it is necessary to take this survey back to some works written before the council.

The best starting point for our discussion of the 'ecclesiology of communion' would seem to be the sacramental ontology of Y. Congar. He puts the stress on aspects of sacramental ontology bound up with the sacramental anthropology of episcopal ordination and develops its consequences at the level of collegiality. He seems to be largely influenced not only by the patristic tradition but also by ecumenical motives, in particular: history, liturgical life, spirituality and the theology of the Eastern church.[5]

In 1961 Karl Rahner was still stressing the importance of the local church, though he did not always decisively relate the figure of the bishop to the particular church or diocese, which in his view is ultimately most important. The theme of the particular church/universal church is given a deeper organic interpretation, for example, in the 'eucharistic ecclesiology' of J. Ratzinger, and some of its aspects are also indicated by G. Dejaifve. Although the two authors differ at some points of their discussion, they agree in stressing the eucharist and the mystical body, in co-ordinating them, and in seeing them as basic reasons for the reciprocal integration of unity and multiplicity. It is worth noting Ratzinger's stress on brotherhood. This is an indispensable factor in understanding the figure of the bishop and grasping the concept that the episcopal college 'represents the church'.

One attempt at theological precision relating to our discussion can also be found in the document *Select Themes of Ecclesiology*, produced by the International Theological Commission.[6] The distinction between the particular church, which is primarily the diocese, and the local church, as the totality of particular churches, and between the 'essential structure' of the church and its 'concrete and changing form', and the theological space given to the category of 'ecclesial communion', are basic advances which condition episcopal collegiality. It seems useful to connect this document with some of the theological research of A. Antón, H. Legrand and W. Kasper.

In his writings the ecclesiologist A. Antón often speaks of episcopal collegiality. Thus his important report to the 1969 Synod of Bishops begins from the theology of communion, communion among the faithful, hierarchical communion, and communion within the episcopal college; it continues with the theology of the particular church.[7] His theological survey of the period after the council relates specifically to the church as a mystery of communion and as the *communio ecclesiarum*, and it is on this that he bases his reflections on the institutional structures of the church, including those on the primate and the episcopal college. Legrand offers a broad discussion of the local church: he tries to specify the ways in which it relates to the bishop and the episcopal college, and stresses the need to exclude an approach in which the first question is that of the particular church or the universal church. There is in fact a degree of perichoresis, of reciprocity, between the two.[8] Kasper pays a good deal of attention to the category of 'communion' and, among other things, firmly stresses that according to the Catholic church, the particular church essentially means openness to all the other particular churches and to the universal church, and therefore also to the papacy.[9] It seems to me that while these emphases demonstrate the opposition between a so-called 'universalist ecclesiology' and the 'ecclesiology of communion', they could be reconciled with a discussion which, while starting from the universal church, would succeed in integrating into its proposal the essential instances of the theological element of the 'particular church'.

Because of their importance for collegiality also, it is worth noting the ecumenically committed contributions by E. Lanne and by J. M. R. Tillard. The former stresses the particular church/local church and the eucharistic/*communio* ecclesiology with emphases which bear witness to his deep knowledge of Orthodoxy, producing figures of the primate and the episcopate which contain innovative elements in continuity with authentic tradition. The latter, stressing recent biblical studies and some elements of patristic thought, tries to make a better connection between the *magisterium* of Vatican I and that of Vatican II, and presents the Petrine service of the Bishop of Rome above all as a significant visible principle of the unity of the *Una Sancta*, and this unity as a communion of churches on the basis of the unity and plurality which is to be found in the Holy Trinity. In this context he offers only a re-reception of episcopal collegiality.[10]

A number of authors have investigated the reasons for this theological interest in episcopal collegiality in the years during and after Vatican II.

Despite the variety of opinions, this has been identified as lying in the theology of the local church, in the rediscovery of the sacramentality of the episcopate, in the symbolic and eschatological conception of the apostolic succession, in the issue of mission and in the revival of the 'ecclesiology of communion'. In my view the last proposal seems to be the best.

3. Sacramental foundations of episcopal collegiality

The fact of the sacramentality of the episcopate is clearly affirmed by Vatican II. However, there is no unanimity as to how what the council says is related to it. One might take as an example the way in which the power of jurisdiction is conferred on the bishop. Even after the council there are those like G. Ghirlanda, who argues, following the line of e.g. C. Journet, D. Staffa and A. Gutierrez, that this power is conferred on the bishop directly by the pope.[11] Other authors, however, do not find these arguments convincing. Thus in the text of St Leo the Great (*Ep.* 10 to the bishops of the province of Vienne, in 445, PL 54, 629), it is necessary to distinguish between the conferring of the power of jurisdiction and *missio canonica*: the pope intervenes at this second level. So Ghirlanda's interpretation of the texts of Leo the Great and the *Nota explicativa praevia* in connection with this problem do not help. Expert interpreters like W. Bertrams, U. Betti, C. Colombo and G. Philips rule out such exegesis. The same authors, and others, like Congar and Hamer, show that to deny that the pope confers the episcopal power of jurisdiction is not tantamount to taking away some of his primatial power as defined at Vatican I.

These somewhat negative observations have been supplemented, in post-conciliar theology, with positive statements. These assert that the sacrament of ordination, through inclusion in the succession of the apostolic ministry, creates an essential relationship between the bishop and both the episcopal college and the particular church; in this context there is increasing reflection on the concept of the 'representation' not only of Christ but also of the particular church and, through the college, of the whole church. Without failing to recognize the juridical dimension of episcopal collegiality, noted in a balanced way in many theological and juridical works like that of W. Bertrams, one cannot but notice a certain 'fragility' of effect at the operative level. Leaving aside the position of K. Rahner, which, referring to the pope, adapts the fullness of the powers received in the sacrament of ordination to the special ministry exercised by the church,[12] the opportunity is taken to found and duly to co-ordinate the power of order and the power of jurisdiction or 'pastoral' power in episcopal ministry. It is worth noting that the sacramental powers of the bishop are also a 'structure' of the church in that they are a structural sign of the essential dimension of service, of the church and in the church.

4. Communion and law in the episcopal college

In the expression 'episcopal college', the term 'college' indicates a group of unequal persons. Moreover, the episcopal college succeeds the apostolic college by the will of Christ. Furthermore, there is a proportional relationship between the apostolic college and the episcopal college. Finally, sacramental consecration is the cause of inclusion in the episcopal college; hierarchical communion is its necessary condition. These are, I would say, eirenic affirmations. Others, however, are not. Here are some examples. In coming to terms with the contrast between the different positions it may sometimes be encouraging to remember the comment by H. de Lubac that episcopal collegiality should not be shaped on the basis of 'prefabricated models'.[13]

There are authors who ask themselves whether episcopal consecration makes the bishop first a member of the episcopal college and then, as a result, the head of a particular church or whether he is first the head of a particular church and then, as a result, a member of the episcopal college. As far as I can see, since the council there have been three answers to this question. The first is that of people like E. Schillebeeckx, U. Betti, W. Onclin, H. de Lubac and Karl Rahner himself, despite his position in defence of the local church, who affirm the priority of the episcopal college over the particular church: there are in fact bishops who are not bishops of a diocese. A second hypothesis is that of L. Bouyer, who seems to follow the Eastern solution, which argues the priority of the particular church over the college. The third position of that of H. Legrand and, it seems, the final standpoint of Y. Congar: these argue that there is no theological foundation to the discussion as to whether the episcopal college or the particular church has priority, because of the special 'mutual presence' of the particular church in the whole church and vice versa, according to the ecclesiology of communion.[14] This is the opinion that I prefer.

Another problem is that of the discovery of the best forms of balance in the episcopal college between what I would call the 'monarchical' principle and the 'collegial' principle. This brings out the importance of co-ordinating the legal aspect within the ecclesial communion, i.e. the relationship between the powers, with the moral aspect, or with an action which, in order to respect the multiplicity of gifts and institutions in the church, in fact tends towards prudence. It is well known that the individual bishops must exercise ministry responsibly in their particular church, and be co-responsible at the level of the universal church. It is also clear that the Petrine ministry of the Bishop of Rome is *ad aedificationem Ecclesiae*, and exists for the promotion, in the unity of faith and love, of the personal creativity of his brothers in the episcopate and – leaving aside their theological status here – of the intermediary bodies between the universal church and the particular or diocesan church. These are instances which are difficult to put into practice, above all in certain situations, problems often studied not only by theologians but also by canon lawyers and historians.

Without wanting to enter into the merits of each of them, and without wanting to exclude other names, I would refer for example to H. U. von Balthasar, G. Philips, K. Rahner, J. Ratzinger, H. de Lubac, Y. Congar, J. Hamer, A. Antón, G. Thils, W. Kasper, P. Parente, J. M. R. Tillard, A. Dulles, H. Legrand, W. Bertrams, J. Tomko, V. Fagiolo, C. Colombo, F. J. Saraiva Martins, G. Alberigo, J. Lecuyer, H. J. Pottmeyer, James H. Provost, G. Mucci, S. Dianich, A. Garuti and G. Mazzoni. Apart from some rare interventions which are manifestly polemic, it would appear that their reading of the relationship in the episcopal college between the pope and the other members is moving increasingly closer to the recognition of the presence of a reciprocal effort towards communion and co-participation.

The pope is the head of the episcopal college as 'successor', in the apostolic ministry, to Peter, who is head of the college of the apostles. As head of the college he is relative to the other bishops, who are members of the same college. In their identity as members of the college, vice versa, the bishops are related to and subordinate to the pope. The function and primatial authority of the head, based on a particular charism, are 'personal', for the training of the episcopal college in its legal plenitude. Therefore no decision of the episcopate has the status of a collegial act in the strict sense without at least the implicit will of the pope. Taking into account the divine law and natural law, he can intervene freely in the church for the good of the church.

So regardless of what answer is given to the question whether the primacy of the bishop of Rome is that of his quality as head of the college or as head of the church and vicar of Christ – Paul VI, according to Congar, is said to have interpreted his primacy in terms of his being head of the church – and simply recognizing the value of G. Thils' discussion of the form, the 'limit' and the exercise of the Roman primacy, for the good of the church there is also a need really to allow space for the free and rapid 'personal' intervention of the pope.[15] This would happen mostly where other formulae would not in fact prove effective.

Consequently, even if it must be remembered that there is always a distinction in the person of the Bishop of Rome between the bishop of the city of Rome, the primate of Italy, the patriarch of the West and the pope, and even if it must be noted that in the past there have sometimes been forms of centralism which have harmed the exercise of the Petrine service no less than the churches themselves, it is nevertheless reasonable to affirm that a central organization, suitable for mediating effectively the action of the one who presides over the universal church in love, has to exist and has to function. The history of the early church provides ample evidence not only of the spirit but also of the 'means' of communion between the churches. Just as there is no true unity without real plurality, so there is no true plurality without real unity, and therefore without a real universal structure and real unitary animation. That is important because today in the church, on the basis of a deeper ecclesial awareness and under the stimulus of non-theological factors, which are rightly bringing about more richness, more variety, more diversity, there is particular need for the universal service of unity and for an efficient correlative organization and a general respect for catholicity. Only in this way will the history and the life of the church, through the pluriformity of gifts and charisms, of prophecies of ministries and of cultures, increasingly prove to be a 'creation' of the Holy Spirit and a proof, in time and space, of a marvellous ecumene of individual and collective historical subjects.

5. Supreme authority and its subjects

Are there one or two subjects or organs of supreme authority, of supreme power in the church? This is not, as sometimes appears, the most important problem for episcopal collegiality. Two brief comments will introduce the examination of theological positions on this point.

For the communion which exists between the members of the episcopal college incautious talk of 'first' and 'then', of 'absolutely' and 'exclusively', is not theologically convincing. In describing the logic of the relationship between the head and the other members of the college, writers talk of a degree of complementarity; obviously reciprocity in the strict sense is excluded. Moreover a distinction is made between supreme authority in the church, the subjects and organs which are its vehicles, and the ways in which it is exercised.

Supreme authority can only be one; two supreme authorities are inconceivable in a single social reality. As for the subjects of supreme authority in the church, theologically there are tenable and untenable positions. The former are conciliarist and episcopalist: according to them the supreme visible authority in the church resides in the totality of bishops assembled in council; the pope himself is subject to them. The latter are papalist and curialist, and according to them only the pope has supreme authority in the church; the bishops receive it from him. All the tenable positions affirm that there is one subject of supreme authority, i.e. the college of bishops; however, this exercises its supreme authority in two ways: either through the college (or the pope and the bishops), or through the pope as formally the head of the college – and therefore (authors stress) by an act which is still a collegial act. What is the reason for this position? It is analogous to that adopted over the uniqueness of supreme authority: two subjects bearing the same supreme power are inconceivable in one social reality. After K. Rahner, the representatives of this position ae, for example, T. I. Jimenez Urresti, G. Thils, A. Antón, O. Semmelroth, E. Schillebeeckx, C. Duquoc, C. Butler, P. Rusch, H. Legrand, B. Gherardini, R. P. McBrien and, if I am not mistaken, Y. Congar. However, for example J. Hamer, U. Betti, A. Auer, W. Bertrams, K. Mörsdorf and F. Frost assert that there are two subjects of supreme ministerial authority in the church which are not adequately distinguished, the pope on the one hand and the pope and the other members of the episcopal college on the other.[16]

It seems that both possible solutions have advantages and disadvantages. For the sake of simplicity it might be said that the former stresses the pole of the episcopate but is less happy in stressing the particular charism of the Petrine service. The latter is the opposite. Vatican II, going by the majority of interpreters, leaves matters open. In the present *quaestio libere disputata* I personally am in favour of the solution which holds that there is a single subject of supreme authority in the church and there are two distinct ways of exercising it. In this solution, too, the discussion in Catholic theology, critical and ecclesial, succeeds in fully safeguarding the dogmatic dignity and the free exercise of the supreme pastoral ministry of the Bishop of Rome. However, the ultimate guarantee of a real balance between the personal and the collegial exercise of supreme authority in the church will be the Holy Spirit and in him, the disciples of Christ, in praise of God and in service of men and women.

6. Forms of episcopal collegiality

Not infrequently the assertion can be found that the exercising of episcopal collegiality is one of the most significant contexts for checking how Vatican II has been received. This is true. However, it is important to remember that a critical awareness of the post-conciliar reception of episcopal collegiality entails the full awareness not only of consensus but also of problems relating to terminology and content. Given that ways of exercising of collegiality seem to be part of our argument, for the sake of completeness I shall discuss them. However, since others have discussed them at length, I shall be brief.

First of all, theologically there is agreement in thinking that a collegial action in the real and proper sense of the word, and therefore in the full sense, comes about through the defining action of an ecumenical council. The International Theological Commission affirms the possibility of a collegial action in the full sense also 'in the unitary action of the bishops who reside in different parts of the world'. Its effective existence depends on the presence of the formal and legal dimension of communion with the pope. According to this Commission, only the synod of bishops, because it is in some sense representative of all the Catholic bishops, can be a partial but true form of episcopal collegiality. For the same reason, conferences of bishops cannot have this role. These and their continental groupings are not of divine law and therefore do not *per se* exercise an ecclesiastical *magisterium*. They are useful, indeed necessary, but only for realizing '"together" or "conjointly" some of their apostolic and pastoral responsibilities'.[17]

Other theologians take a different line in their attempt to deepen and develop conciliar teaching. This is what led, in the case of the Synod of Bishops, to the promotion of an effective representation of all the episcopate and therefore a formally collegial decision-making process, obviously *cum et sub* the head of the episcopal college. There are still those, like A. Antón, who speak of the theological foundation of the conferences of bishops, of their theological form as an intermediate authority between the diocesan bishop and the episcopal college – while avoiding dangers which have been rightly denounced[18] – and of their capacity as an ordinary ecclesiastical *magisterium*.[19]

A theological evaluation is not easy here. On the one hand, if it is argued that the action of the episcopal college in the strict sense in principle relates to the whole episcopate and the whole church, there is only a real and proper collegiality where this can be demonstrated. It can therefore be asked whether an episcopal collegiality which is not such is not just analogical and improper. It should be noted that the answer should not be decided on the basis of general formal content, of categories, of adjectival descriptions, but by taking account of the real content which is assumed in the discussion. On the other hand, simply putting it on a different theological and juridical level, it is not evident how there cannot also be a real but partial collegiality. It is certainly necessary to continue to study the problem.

John-Paul II also rightly stresses the *affectus collegialis*, the collegial spirit. This is as it were the heart of any form of episcopal collegiality, from collegiality in the strict sense, in the full sense, to the action of the college of cardinals, the activity of the Roman Curia and *ad limina* visits. It is also as it were the heart of that extraordinary pastoral form represented by the apostolic visits of the Bishop of Rome. On the *affectus collegialis* ultimately depends the future effectiveness of episcopal collegiality itself. Within a correct relationship between unity and catholicity, by the action of the Holy Spirit and by paying attention to history and to cultures, the collegial spirit will be able to promote the current forms of collegiality and invent new ones. In fact episcopal collegiality needs to be thought of in essentially dynamic terms. It is needed as the solution to the relationship between the particular church and the universal church along the lines of the ecclesiology of communion.

Translated by John Bowden

Notes

1. Cf. Richard P. McBrien, 'Collegiality: State of the Question', in *The Once and Future Church: A Communion of Freedom, Studies on Unity and Collegiality in the Church*, ed. James A. Coriden, Staten Island, NY 1971, 1, 21.

2. Cf. J. Ratzinger, *Das neue Volk Gottes. Entwürfe zur Ekklesiologie*, Düsseldorf 1969 (I have referred to the Italian translation, *Il nuovo popolo di dio. Questioni ecclesiologiche*, Brescia 1971, 224f.).

3. Cf. G. Colombo, 'Risposta alla relazione di R. Sobansky', in *Natura e futuro delle conferenze episcopali. Atti del Colloquio internazionale di Salamanca (3–8 gennaio 1988)*, ed. H. Legardan, J. Manzanares and A. Garcia y Garcia, Bologna 1981, 118 (there is also a Spanish edition).

4. Cf. J. A. Komonchak, 'La sussidiarietà nella chiesa: stato della questione', in *Natura e futuro* (n.3), 321–69.

5. Yves M.-J. Congar, *Ministères et Communion ecclésiale*, Paris 1971; see also his introduction to *La collégialité épiscopale. Histoire et théologie*, Paris 1965. For episcopal collegiality in Congar, Ratzinger and Bertrams see G. Mazzoni, *La collegialità*

episcopale tra teologia e diritto canonico, Bologna 1986 (with bibliographies on the three authors).

6. See Commissio Theologica Internationalis, *Themata selecta de ecclesiologia occasione XX anniversarii conclusionis concilii oecumenici Vaticani II*, Vatican City 1985, 30f., 35–8.

7. A. Antón, *Primado y colegialidad. Sus relaciones a la luz del primer Sínodo extraordinario*, Madrid 1970, 27–94.

8. Cf. H. Legrand, 'La réalisation de l'Église en un lieu', *Initiation à la pratique de la théologie*, ed. B. Lauret and F. Refoulé, Vol. III, *Dogmatique*, Paris 1983, 143–345.

9. Cf. *Zukunft aus der Kraft des Konzils. Die ausserordentliche Bischofssynode '85. Die Dokumente mit einem Kommentar von W. Kasper*, Freiburg 1986, 91; W. Kasper, 'Das Petrusamt als Dienst der Einheit. Die Lehre des I. und II. Vatikanischen Konzils und die gegenwärtige Diskussion', *Das Papstamt, Dienst oder Hindernis für die Ökumene?*, Regensburg 1985, 113–38.

10. J. M. R. Tillard, *L'évêque de Rome*, Paris 1982; *Église d'Églises. L'ecclésiologie de communion*, Paris 1987, passim. Cf. B. Forte, *La Chiesa icona della Trinità. Breve ecclesiologia*, Rome 1984, 44–59.

11. G. Ghirlanda, '*Hierarchica communio*'. *Significato della formula nella 'Lumen Gentium'*, Rome 1980.

12. K. Rahner defends and develops his position in *Nuovi Saggi*, Vol. I, Rome 1968, 509–15.

13. Cf. H. de Lubac, *Les Églises particulières dans l'Église universelle*, Paris 1971 (I have consulted the Italian edition, *Pluralismo di Chiese o unità della Chiesa?*, Brescia 1973, 66).

14. Cf. at least Congar, *Ministères* (n.5: I have consulted the Italian edition, *Ministeri e communione ecclesiale*, Bologna 1973, 105–20).

15. See Congar's review in *RSPT* 71, 1987, 159, of *Primauté et collégialité. Le dossier de Gérard Philips sur la Nota Explicativa Praevia*, ed. J. Grootaers, Louvain 1986.

16. Of all these authors, I would mention at least the works of J. Hamer, 'I soggetti della suprema potestà nella Chiesa: visione teologica', *Il nuovo codice di diritto canonica. Novità, motivazione e significato*, Rome 1983, 139–49.

17. Cf. Commissio Theologica, *Themata selecta* (n.6), 32–5. See the different theological positions in *La collegialità episcopale per il futuro della Chiesa*, ed. V. Fagiolo and G. Concetti, Florence 1969, 3–78, and in *Sinodo dei Vescovi, Natura, metodo, prospettive*, ed. J. Tomko, Vatican City 1985.

18. Cf. *Rapporto sulla fede. Vittorio Messori a colloquio con il car. J. Ratzinger*, Cinisello (Mi) 1985, 55–70.

19. See A. Antón, *Conferencias episcopales ¿Instancias intermedias? El estado teológico de la cuestión*, Salamanca 1989. Cf. also *Die Bischofskonferenz. Theologischer und juridischer Status*, ed. H. Müller and H. J. Pottmeyer, Düsseldorf 1989; G. Alberigo, 'Istituzione per la communione tra l'episcopato universale e il vescovo di Roma', *Cristianesimo nella Storia* 2, 1981, 235–66; A. Garuti, *La collegialità oggi e domani*, Bologna 1982; P. Granfield, *The Limits of the Papacy. Authority and Autonomy in the Church*, New York 1987, 77–106.

Implications for Church Law of the Use of the Term 'Collegiality' in the Theological Context of Official Church Statements

Remigiusz Sobański

Methodological considerations

Collegiality is one of the terms used to denote an ecclesial reality. It is therefore an ecclesiological – and thus a theological – term. It proved possible to apply it to the church when the understanding of it in early Christianity was rediscovered. Here the term *collegium* was freed from any association with the *societias aequalium* which still terrified the fathers of the First Vatican Council. Like all theological terms, in church usage the term, which comes from legal language, takes on a modified content analogous to the situation outside the church. The use of a term in no way means that its immanent legal content is taken into account. Again, it is often a long way from insight into this content to a positive acceptance of it. The legal contents of theological terms are subject to a continuous process of their recognition and articulation. But this process is in no way a linear one. Legal terms are not established in a purely deductive way, not least because theological statements often have an open character. The discussion in the council *aula* and at the 1969 Synod of Bishops showed that views are divided over the legal implications of collegiality. So when elucidating the legal content of ecclesiological terms we may not work with fixed legal conceptions. The system of interpersonal communication underlying the structures of the church cannot always be expressed and shaped with the conceptuality developed in other spheres of law (the concept of the *collegium* is an example of this). Moreover, we have to take into account that even in the church sphere, the same term does not always have the same content.

The concept of collegiality

According to the teaching of Vatican II the content of the term collegiality is the fact that 'just as, in accordance with the Lord's decree, St Peter and the rest of the apostles constitute a unique apostolic college, so in like fashion the Roman Pontiff, Peter's successor, and the bishops, the successors of the apostles, are related with and united to one another' (*Lumen Gentium* 22.1). So collegiality denotes the 'collegial nature and character of the episcopate'. In the Constitution *Lumen Gentium* and the Decree *Christus Dominus* the essential legal implications of collegiality are explained, namely obtaining membership of the episcopal college, the role of the head, the supreme and full authority of the college and the conditions and natures of its exercise (*Lumen Gentium* 22.2; *Christus Dominus* 4). These implications are also discussed in the 'explanatory comments'.

Starting from the 'collegial nature and character of the episcopate', the council states that collegial unity also appears in the reciprocal relationships of the individual bishops to the particular churches and to the whole church (*Lumen Gentium* 23.1). It also draws the practical conclusion that the conferences of bishops can 'contribute in many and fruitful ways to the concrete realization of the collegiate spirit' (*Lumen Gentium* 23.4). This statement suggests that collegiality is grounded in the fact that the bishops form a college, but as a characteristic of the episcopate is not just limited to acts of the episcopal college – in the sense of its totality along with the head. So collegiality as a property of the office of bishop is seen by the council both in the vertical and in the horizontal dimension. This leaves the way open to seeing collegiality in the broader ecclesial context. This direction is taken both in the statements of the *magisterium* and in the literature after the council.[2]

The concept of collegiality is associated above all with that of communion. In his allocution at the opening of the Extraordinary Synod of Bishops in 1969 Paul VI stressed that collegiality is none other than *quaedam communio*.[3] In this description of collegiality, moreover, such terms are used as *animorum coniunctio, fraternitas, unitas, caritas* – all with the verb *est*.[4] The bishops are called *fratres, confratres, collegae*. According to Paul VI episcopal collegiality is a special expression of church *communio*: in the community of bishops *communio* is developed as collegiality[5] and there takes on greater fullness because the bishops are heirs to all the titles and tasks given to the apostles.[6] The association of collegiality with the concept of *communio* is strongly stressed in the closing report of the 1985 synod of bishops: the ecclesiology of *communio* gives collegiality a sacramental basis (II C 4). It was clear that one may not reduce '*communio* ecclesiology to questions and problems of pure organization which relate to powers in the church'. But it was equally clear that 'the *communio* ecclesiology forms the basis for order in the church and specially for rights in their ongoing relationship between unity and multiplicity' (II C 1). The 'theological' and 'legal' views may not part company, nor may one be played off against the other.

The same is true of collegiality as an expression of *communio* at the episcopal level. 'The theology of collegiality is essentially more comprehensive than a purely legal approach' (II C 4). However, this statement may not conceal the fact that as a 'characteristic of the episcopate', and thus as a special expression of *communio*, collegiality by nature also has legal implications and that one cannot appropriately speak of collegiality without taking account of them.

The legal implications also stand in the background to the distinction between affective and effective collegiality.[7] However, this distinction easily leads to the temptation to reduce collegiality in the true sense of the word to effective collegiality and to deny affective collegiality legal consequences.[8] We find examples of such an understanding of collegiality in the 1985 document of the International Theological Commission[9] and in the Roman draft on the conferences of bishops.[10]

On the other hand this decision allows the concept of collegiality to be used even when it has been legally undermined and means only an 'indeterminate feeling'.

Behind the distinction between effective and affective collegiality there is in fact a legitimate concern, namely a concern to characterize clearly a formal act of the episcopal college, but it transpires that this opens up the way both to a narrowing of the concept and to so great an extension of it that it is almost emptied of content. However, affective collegiality may 'not be understood as a purely emotional entity, as merely a collegial disposition'.[11] As an expression of ontological and sacramental reality it forms the basis of effective collegiality, just as *communio* – of which collegiality is the expression – forms an 'organic reality which takes on a legal form and at the same time is ensouled by love' (*Nexpr* 2).

The use of the term 'collegiality'

What significance is to be attached to the term 'collegiality' in official church statements after the council? In investigating this question we can leave on one side statements relating to the ecumenical council, because there is no doubt that collegiality effectively finds its realization in the council. In post-conciliar statements forms of the realization of collegiality mentioned are:[12] the synod of bishops, the college of cardinals, the conferences of bishops, the particular councils, the Roman Curia, the pastoral visits of the pope and *ad limina* visits. In the closing report of the 1985 synod of bishops these forms are ranked as real but partial realizations of collegiality, and it is also said that they are not to be derived directly from the theological principle of collegiality, but are regulated by church law (II C 4). This can only mean, however, that these forms do not compelling arise out of collegiality, for – on the one hand – the ecumenical council is also an institution 'regulated' by church law and – on the other hand – as partial realizations of collegiality they do not form alien bodies in the church which would lack a theological foundation. The question is therefore not whether they necessarily arise out of collegiality, but what is meant by the term 'collegiality', if these institutions are presented as its realization.

In order to clarify the meaning of the term collegiality in the context of these institutions it seems necessary to compare these statements with their legal status in the new Code. I shall begin with the 'pre-conciliar' institutions. Here it is to be noted that the fact that an institution was already active before the 'discovery' of collegiality does not stand in the way of its being understood as a form of the realization of collegiality, for the canonical institutions usually develop before their theological foundation has been clarified. The question is, however, how far their collegial aspect is reflected in the new law and in what sense this institution is to be understood as a realization of collegiality.

1. The college of cardinals. This is listed under the *signa collegialitatis*. Its association with the pope's service to the universal church is grounded not only in the historical role of the college but in the development of collegiality. It is stressed that the revaluation of the college of cardinals does not obscure the collegial character of the service of the episcopate but brings it even more clearly to light.[13] The service of the college of cardinals is denoted both in papal statements and in canon 349 as assistance in the daily care of the universal church. This aspect of the universal church is stressed with a reference to the composition of the college, and its relationship to the exercise of episcopal collegiality with reference to the summoning of the consistory.[14]

2. According to canon 360, the Roman Curia is an institution 'by which the pope conducts the business of the universal church'. The inclusion of

some diocesan bishops was mentioned by Paul VI as a sign of the furthering of collegiality.[15] Although the Roman Curia is often simply mentioned among the realizations of collegiality, this is made more precise in the Constitution *Pastor bonus*, which says that the Roman Curia is distinguished by a certain degree of collegiality and cannot be compared to any other collegial institution. Alongside the role which determines the view of it as a direct instrument of the pope, the constitution also notes the service of the Curia to the episcopal college.[16] There is also reference to a 'collegiality *sui generis*' within the Curia, which rests on the devoted collaboration and co-responsibility of all in its service.[17]

3. The regulations of canons 399–400 in the 1983 Codex about *ad limina* visits correspond to canons 340–341 in the 1917 codex. Within the horizons of collegiality this duty of the bishops is interpreted as a reciprocal enrichment: of the pope by the bishops, and the bishops above all in individual conversations and collegial meetings.[18] Both the pope and the bishops strengthen one another in the awareness that they are not alone.[19] The same significance is attached to the pastoral visits of the Bishop of Rome: they are said to stress the place of the local churches in the universal church and to do so against the background of the brotherhood of all humankind.[20]

4. From the day on which the synod of bishops was introduced, there was repeated and strong stress that it is an effective expression of the collegiality of the episcopate.[21] Despite the clear statements about the synod as a realization of collegiality, in the literature views on this are divided. Other contributions in this issue relate to the synod; here I shall simply point out that neither in the *motu proprio Apostolica sollicitudo* nor in canons 342–348 is the term 'episcopal college' to be found, and that – on the other hand – in the article on the episcopal college (canons 336–341), but above all in canon 337.2 (which mentions the extra-conciliar acts of the episcopal college), the synod is not mentioned.

5. 'The meaning of collegiality is concretely realized in the conferences of bishops.'[22] But in the 1985 declaration of the Theological Commission and in the 'Roman draft' of 1987 it is asserted that in connection with the conferences one 'can speak of collegiality' only 'in an analogous and theologically inauthentic sense'.

6. In the course of a revival of collegiality the particular councils and other forms of collegial collaboration of the bishops are discussed – e.g. within the major world cities.[23]

The term collegiality is also used without reference to concrete institutions. It denotes a (collegial) disposition which is meant to inspire the activity of the bodies that are addressed. Thus in the bull which promulgates the 1983 codex it is stressed 'with all clarity' that it was worked out 'in an outstandingly collegial spirit' and that 'this note of collegiality eminently characterizes and distinguishes the process of its development'. While its promulgation is an act of pontifical authority and therefore has 'primatial character', in substance it reflects 'the collegial sollicitude' of the bishops and 'should be considered the fruit of a collegial collaboration because of the efforts on the part of specialized persons and institutions throughout the whole church'.[24] In the modern world any codification is the result of the collaboration of specialized persons. Therefore the term collegiality in this context can no longer denote a sense of responsibility which is to be shared by all believers.[25]

This survey shows clearly that collegiality always primarily means the *affectus collegialis*. It determines the attitude of *communio*, and in *communio* the *affectus* is 'the soul of collaboration between bishops at a regional, national and international level'.[26] But if this were all, the term collegiality would not be necessary at all; there would be no need of a modern word, for an attitude corresponding to affective collegiality has been displayed by churchmen down the centuries who did not know this term. Rather, its use is meant to root the content which it denotes more deeply in the consciousness and to contribute towards its realization. Therefore the popes stress to the bishops that collegiality is not only affective but at the same time effective.[27]

The council debates were about this effective collegiality, and because of its legal consequences the term 'collegiality' prevailed (and also caused difficulties). That from the beginning this was a term fraught with legal implications is also evident from the fact that the Synod of Bishops – as one of the forms of the realization of collegiality – was announced on the opening day of the last period of the council (14 September 1965) and was established the next day. But this fact also shows that whenever there is mention of collegiality in the context of various institutions, what is referred to is not only an affective collegiality (which should never be lacking) but effective collegiality and its legal implications. The 'old' institutions are no less emphasized as a realization of collegiality than the synod of bishops or conferences of bishops.

For all the affirmation of the realization of collegiality in these institutions it is, however, conceded that in this respect they can be improved. Both Paul VI[28] and John-Paul II[29] said this of the Synod of Bishops; the service of the college of cardinals is seen in a new light,[30] and the Roman Curia was reformed twice even before the council. The question is still how the legal consequences of collegiality can effectively be put into practice: solidarity (of bishops with the pope and the pope with the bishops), shared responsibility, the duty to collaborate at various levels, are still enjoined – and rightly so, for as an ecclesial reality all this is the object of church teaching, of stimulus, encouragement and instruction. At the same time, however, it is the task of church law to establish institutions which make it possible to accede to this co-responsibility.

The legal understanding

However, the collegial disposition needs help from both sides. The college of cardinals, the diocesan bishops included in the Roman Curia, help the pope in the exercise of his service to the universal church; the *ad limina* visits and the pastoral visits of the pope provide help for the bishops. But collegiality as a characteristic of the episcopate means far more. From it there follows a co-responsibility for the universal church which the bishops, apart from their contribution as leaders of their (particular) churches, 'for the good of the whole mystical body', assume not only through a strictly collegial act at the ecumenical council, but also in another way, albeit 'not by an act of jurisdiction' (*Lumen Gentium* 23.2).

Institutions which are to secure more than the guarantee of support given in a collegial spirit must take account of the *iunctim* between the primatial and the collegial principle,[31] and in so doing note that although the episcopal college is not always 'fully active', all bishops by virtue of their consecration are always and constantly obliged to be concerned for the universal church and to bear responsibility for it.

No one doubts that legally the primatial principle is completely safeguarded both at the ecumenical council and also in all the institutions provided for in the perspective of collegiality. The collegial principle found its legal implementation in the advisory function at the level of the universal church – apart from the ecumenical council. There are institutions to which the pope does not belong and which – like the synod of bishops, the 'most effective instrument of collegiality' – are ultimately the auxiliary organs of the Bishop of Rome.[32]

Here we reach the limits of law. Beyond question the existing institutions can be improved; one can rightly raise the question of the organisms which provide collegial support [33] and pin hopes on a legal application of a deepened doctrine of the *communio ecclesiarum*, but without reflecting on the available legal categories one cannot arrive at the *cum Petro et sub Petro* without falling into one-sided solutions, solutions which do not fully correspond to ecclesial reality. Apart from the council, at which the episcopal college exercises its authority in solemn form (*Lumen Gentium* 22.2), all institutions intended as a realization of collegiality are imprisoned in the alternative of making decisions or offering advice, and because of the primatial principle they can only be instruments for offering advice. But however important advice may be, the meaning of collegiality does not lie here. The episcopal college does not stand over against the pope but works *una cum capite*.

The starting point for the legal expression of collegiality should not be fear of a limitation of competence but the collegial disposition. The theological and legal views of collegiality should not fall apart, for example in the sense that the theological view embraces the disposition whereas in the legal view questions of power predominate. The theology of collegiality must be always concerned with the legal implications, and juristic thought must begin with ecclesial reality. If theological thought and thought in terms of church law begin from different approaches, there is a danger that theology will become vague and law will be ecclesially undermined. The dichotomy of theological and canonical thought leads to the formation of institutions which cannot do full justice to ecclesial reality: theological data are developed by means of legal categories which derive from another sphere and with which the object to be regulated cannot be grasped. It is not a matter of a juristic working over of ecclesial reality, but of the comprehension of its legal content.

Collegiality, with its *iunctim* between the primatial and the collegial principle, is an instructive example of this. The idea of competence comes to grief on its transformation into law, which ultimately leads inescapably either to the limitation of primacy or the undermining of collegiality. The category of participation, by which competence can be established, would have to come into the foreground. This protects us against thought which isolates law as an interpersonal structure of communication from the values that are communicated. For the expression of collegiality in law ('*communio* at the episcopal level') it is decisive that it rests on a participation in the mission of the whole church and co-responsibility. The voice of the bishops is not to be taken as an expression of opinion or of their will, but as a qualified testimony of faith: of the one faith of the church of Christ lived out by them and their churches. This presumption does not allow us to dismiss the bishops' contribution as advice, and on the other hand it draws its power from the unity of faith, the faith of all the bishops with their head.

It is not difficult to cover the second aspect in law (in the end above all thanks to the primatial principle, since there cannot be any testimony to the faith of the church without the pope or even against him). The transformation of the power of the voice of the bishops into law presents difficulties in the perspective of the universal church. This is attested by the institutional safeguarding of the primatial principle on the one hand and the references to the *affectus collegialis* on the other. Regardless of any view of the institutions functioning today (which are historically conditioned and capable of improvement) there are no difficulties in principle in safeguarding the exercise of the right and duty of free expression of opinion, the exchange of opinion and the formation of a common approach in institutional terms. But no obligation can be laid on the pope to accept this approach. It cannot either be dismissed as advisory or stressed as decisive.

The legal evaluation must begin with the ecclesial significance of testimony. It is a qualified testimony of the pastors in the *communio ecclesiarum*. This *manifestatio sententiae* has its deepest significance not in the ascertaining of facts but in the living process of *traditio* and *receptio*, in which the truth is conveyed, assimilated and related to praxis. Witness contains an appeal for acceptance, but at the same time it is bound up with testimony of the whole college. Here we have the legal claim which is contained in the witness given 'among colleagues'. The claim is based on the obligation of the teacher of faith to the truth and to the hearers of the word. This obligation is borne by all bishops, and therefore the claim cannot be separated from the obligation of a sharing in the formation of a common testimony which is ready to listen and to learn, a testimony which would correspond to the truth and to the needs of the time (both in formulation and in practical effects). That is what the exercise of collegiality is all about. The inalienable service of the bishops in the 'unique accord' (*Dei Verbum* 10) of the *communio ecclesiarum* determines all the institutions of collegiality which have developed in history, from the first synods to their most recent developments. Their significance rests on the fact that collegiality does not remain an abstract or sentimental concept and that its exercise is not dependent on a subjective disposition, but on the effective expression of the *communio ecclesiarum*.

In the legal regulation of the exercise of collegiality we can and should learn from the experience of co-responsibility and co-determination found in political institutions. But limits are set to the evaluation of this experience by the unique nature of the Catholic church, which not only consists of particular churches but at the same time also exists in them (*Lumen Gentium* 23.2).[34] Here too it is evident that the interference of church law and the 'other' law must have different effects. As the church and those of its institutions which we must consider to be *iuris divini* are a gift (of salvation), we should above all look at the developing and encouraging possibilities of law. The realization of collegiality does not come about through compromise or by tailoring the law for one at the expense of another. On the contrary, the realization of collegiality leads through research and proclamation of the rights of the college, i.e. the pope and the other bishops: rights which are grounded in their mission and therefore are tasks and duties orientated on the unity of faith and its historical achievement. Here the laws above all have the role of shaping consciousness, encouraging activity and providing integration.

Positive solutions will always lag behind the ecclesial reality. They are historically conditioned, and the accents also lie in different places (stress on the primatial or collegial principle); moreover, one could also wish that today's solutions were different.[35] For as an expression of *communio*, episcopal collegiality is part of the *mysterium ecclesiae*, the investigation, realization and legal expression of which always remains a task.

Translated by John Bowden

Notes

1. Thus in canon 115, following Ulpian's definition, *collegium* is defined as an aggregate of persons with equal rights, whereas in canon 331 *collegium* is to be understood in terms of its legal definition, which takes up *Lumen Gentium* 22.1.

2. My remarks are limited to collegiality at the level of the universal church.

3. *Allocutio* 11 October 1969: AAS 61, 1969, 717.

4. Ibid.

5. *Allocutio* 12 November 1969: *Osservatore Romano*, 13 November 1969, 1.

6. *Allocutio* 11 October 1969: AAS 61, 1969, 717.

7. G. Alberigo, 'Istituzioni per la communione tra l'episcopato universale e il vescovo di Roma', *Cristianesimo nella Storia* 2, 1981, 235–66: 249f.

8. Ibid.

9. Commissio Theologica Internationalis, *Themata selecta de ecclesiologia*, Libreria Vaticana 1985, 34 (Documenta 13).

10. On this see the contributions in *Die Bischofskonferenz. Theologischer und juridischer Status*, ed. H. Müller and H. J. Pottmeyer, Düsseldorf 1989.

11. W. Kasper, 'Der theologische Status der Bischofskonferenzen', *ThQ* 167, 1987, 1–6:3.

12. E.g. Paul VI's address of 11 October 1969 (n.3); the first encyclical of John-Paul II, *Redemptor hominis* 4 March 1979, no. 5: AAS 71, 1979, 264f., especially the address of 28 June 1980: AAS 72, 1980, 644–55; the report by the Extraordinary Synod of Bishops of 7 December 1985, II C, *Herder Korrespondenz* 40, 1986, 44f.

13. John-Paul II, *Allocutio* of 23 November 1982: AAS 75, 1983, 13f.; *Allocutio* of 26 November 1982: AAS 75, 1983, 143.

14. John-Paul II, *Allocutio* of 28 June 1980: AAS 72, 1980, 647.

15. *Allocutio* of 11 October 1969: AAS 61, 1969, 717.

16. No. 10: AAS 80, 1988, 853.

17. John-Paul II, *Allocutio* of 28 June 1980: AAS 72, 1980, 649.

18. Ibid.

19. John-Paul II, *Allocutio* of 28 May 1982: AAS 74, 1982, 917.

20. John-Paul II, *Allocutio* of 28 June 1980: AAS 72, 1980, 649–51.

21. '*Synodus Episcoporum est singularis excellens ostensio collegialitatis Ecclesiae et eius instrumentum peculiari modo efficax*', John-Paul II, *Allocutio* of 29 October 1983: AAS 76, 1984, 287. Cf. also the addresses by Paul VI, 1 May 1969; *Osservatore Romano* 2–3 May 1969, 2; 11 October 1969; AAS 61, 1969, 717; John-Paul II, 23 November 1982: AAS 75, 1983, 136f.; 26 November 1982: AAS 75, 1983, 142f.

22. Closing report of the 1985 Synod of Bishops, II C 5. Cf. e.g. Paul VI, *Allocutio* of 11 October 1969: AAS 61, 1969, 717; John Paul II, encyclical *Redemptor hominis* no.5; *Allocutio* of 28 June 1980: AAS 72, 1980, 647; 28 May 1982: AAS 74, 1982, 917.

23. John-Paul II, encyclical *Redemptor hominis*, no. 5.

24. *Code of Canon Law*, Latin-English Edition, xii and xiii.

25. In the bull promulgating the 1917 Code the collaboration of many experts is also mentioned, as are the fruits of taking advice from '*cunctorum in Episcopatu venerabilium Fratrum*'.

26. 1985 Synod, Closing Report, II C 4.

27. John-Paul II, *Allocutio* of 15 June 1984: AAS 77, 1985, 54.

28. *Allocutio* of 11 October 1969: AAS 61, 1969, 717.

29. *Allocutio* of 29 October 1983: AAS 76, 1984, 287.

30. John-Paul II, *Allocutio* of 26 November 1982: AAS 75, 1983, 143.

31. John-Paul II, *Allocutio* of 28 June 1980: AAS 72, 1980, 645.

32. A. Acerbi, 'L'ecclesiologia sottesa alle istituzioni ecclesiali postconciliari', *Cristianesimo nella Storia* 2.1, 1981, 203–34: 212-21.

33. Ibid., 221; Alberigo, 'Istituzioni' (n.7), 235–66: 257.

34. K. Rahner, in K. Rahner, J. Ratzinger, *Episkopat und Primat*, Freiburg, Basel and Vienna ²1961, 32; W. Aymans, 'Die *communio ecclesiarum* als Gestaltgesetz der einen Kirche', *Archiv für katholisches Kirchenrecht* 139, 1970, 69–90.

35. E.g. leaving some matters to the not strictly collegial actions of bishops or the partial realizations of collegiality. Cf. the *vota* of the participants in the 1969 synod of bishops (J. Saraiva Martins, 'De collegiali Ecclesiae postconciliaris itinere', *Divus Thomas* (Piacenza) 76, 1973, 3–49: 37–48, and the suggestions e.g. by G. Alberigo, 'Serving the Communion of Churches', *Concilium* 127, 1979, 12–33.

The Catholic Conception of Collegiality from a European Reformed Perspective

Heiner Grote

The term 'collegiality' has found a home in many languages. Astonishingly, however, *collegialitas* has not yet been adopted as a usage in church Latin, although year by year church Latin keeps creating some new words and phrases so as to be capable of continuing to serve as a means of communication in a changing world. Against this background and after a large number of conversations, in this article I shall sum up the way in which the concept is defined.

'Collegial/collegiality' denotes:

A. Membership of a formal group which as a rule consists of a manageable number of members. Membership is obtained through a qualification of profession, discipline, office or the like: this is common to all members and these members usually have equal rights.

B. Some forms of behaviour which are to be regarded as the heart of 'collegial/collegiality', namely a readiness to supplement and help, toleration even in conflict, respect for a president where necessary, silence when the college thinks that necessary, and so on.

C. Beneficial internal collaboration. The occasions for this are particular concerns and demands, works and tasks, rights and duties the wider community from which the members come, by which they are delegated or for which they are active, cannot themselves undertake.

D. The decisions and actions emanating from this formal group. As they are already the basis for the formation of the college and also for its ongoing existence, it is necessary for the members to bring as much agreed knowledge as possible from outside and also to present the decisions, once made, in harmony; for them at least to bear with these decisions; and never attempt to thwart them from outside with the help of informal groups.

This definition of the concept covers many individual phenomena but also has an idealistic element about it. The aim of it is simply to help to guard against high-handedly relating any concepts from the Protestant side, allegedly or actually arising from the Reformation, to the Roman Catholic Church. Really all the necessary guidelines, conceptions and criteria should arise solely from Holy Scripture and the Christian message. The understanding gained from that of the need for human redemption in community will also come to determine church order sooner or later. It is already instructive that Holy Scripture does not have any barren concepts. Those who listen to it will also be given instruction about collegiality.

I shall just hint at that here.

The 'twelve tribes of Israel', each of which receives 'a special blessing' (Gen. 49.28), can easily be understood as a *collegium*. The same is true of the Levites, who received 'no portion nor inheritance with their brothers; the Lord is their inheritance, as the Lord your God said to them' (Deut. 10.9). Important details of the commandments relating to feast days and worship also unmistakably fill out the details of such colleges. Their influence, inwardly and outwardly, where successful, results in a cry of joy: 'Behold, how good and pleasant it is when brothers dwell in unity!' (Ps. 133.1).

The promise 'Where two or three are gathered together in my name, there am I in the midst of them' (Matt. 18.20) refers to the *ek-klesia* generally. But as those who are 'called out', the group is a college. Its task and privilege is to be a small group representing many people, i.e. to become collegially active. It may also produce sub-colleges from its midst and allow these to develop a subsidiary collegiality. And of course there is no more significant Christian archetype for college and collegiality than the community of the apostles of Jesus Christ. Mention might also be made briefly of the Christian doctrine of the Trinity, which not least can serve as the starting point for a meditation on collegiality.

Although the actual word does not appear, collegiality has been a mark of Christianity throughout its history. In particular, synods and councils, curias and chapters, orders, groups of clergy and lay associations have handed down an awareness of collegiality – sometimes in the face of the harshest opposition – and a church life stamped by it.

The structural innovation brought about by the Reformation can be briefly described as follows: it was the experience of the small communities which were coming to life and encountering one another, and the state churches which were formed by them; at the same time it was a deepened experience of collegiality. The Reformation very soon became certain that *episcope*, too, could be, and indeed had to be, exercised collegially. It found a large number of terms and procedures for this: consistories, presbyteries and synods, also ephorates, superintendentships, parishes and chambers. All these institutions were expressions of collegiality, mixed in with other things. Even the chief *episcopus* appointed by the local ruler and the 'emergency bishop' were (deliberately) active only in association with such a collegial *episcope*.

The seventeenth and eighteenth centuries brought developments and changes. On the one hand the systems of state-church law constructed by Samuel Pufendorf (died 1694) and Christoph Matthäus Pfaff (died 1760), which made *collegium* an important theoretical term, came into being. On the other hand Pietism, represented by Philipp Jakob Spener (died 1705) and August Hermann Francke (died 1727), tried to form nuclei of Christian faith and church life which were understood as *collegia* related to praxis. Both provided important new stimuli for the churches of the Reformation. But the Roman Catholic church saw here all the more reason for keeping its distance from all nouns deriving from the root *colleg-*.

The schema *Supremi Pastoris* prepared for the First Vatican Council (though it was not discussed there) contains the anathema: 'Anyone who says that the church is not a perfect society but a *collegium*, or that within bourgeois society, the state, it is subject to worldly power, let him be anathema' (Mansi 51, col.552, canon 10). The 1917 *Codex Iuris Canonici* uses the terms *corpus* and *senatus*, but not *collegia*, as not in keeping with the nature of the church. It uses the term almost only in a technical legal sense as *personae morales collegiales* (which simply means 'association').

After promptings which already began in the 1920s, in the 1950s changes began to take place. The development was not always clear. There were and are counter-movements. That can be seen from the choice of particular terms. But we need to take note of all the statements and developments which in effect relate to collegiality, which further it or do not further it – on many levels and in a variety of spheres. Keeping the everyday life of the church in view and some important explanations and definitions to hand, I shall now describe and evaluate the current situation. In so doing I shall refer both to the documents of the Second Vatican Council and to the 1983 *Code of Canon Law*.

A. The Roman Catholic Church thinks it important that the collegiality which is valid within it shall not come into being without a clear sacramental reference. Collegiality at the lower level presupposes not only baptism (canon 849) but also the sacrament of confirmation (canon 879). On this basis all the Christian faithful (canon 204.1; 208) can and indeed should become members of a variety of formal groups in the church, insofar as they have the necessary qualifications. Even as lay people (canons 207.1; 225.1) – and here men and women largely have equal rights – they nowadays rise to higher bodies of church administration and church jurisdiction. But where the relationship to further sacraments, particularly to the sacrament of marriage, is not maintained as the church wishes, it has made provisions under church law and the law of contracts for those involved as a result to be disqualified from collegiality in the church.

Collegiality takes on the dimension of consecration as soon as 'sacred ministers, who are also called clerics in law' (207.1) shape it either partially or as a whole. The sacrament of orders (canon 1008) and the incardination associated with it (canon 265) lead to collegiality in particular spheres and at higher levels. A body of priests to be formed in every diocese and whom the bishop is to hear as a duty represents the clergy and furthers the welfare of that 'portion of the people of God' (canon 495.1).

Bishops receive 'the fullness of the sacrament of Orders' (*Lumen Gentium* 21). Therefore the order (*ordo*) or body (*corpus*) formed by the bishops has since the Second Vatican Council also explicitly been called a *collegium*. 'Just as, in accordance with the Lord's decree, St Peter and the rest of the apostles constitute a unique apostolic college, so in like fashion the Roman Pontiff, Peter's successor, and the bishops, the successors of the apostles, are related with and united to one another' (*Lumen Gentium* 22). For all time, this college has been endowed with 'a special outpouring of the Holy Spirit coming upon them'. 'Episcopal consecration confers, together with the office of sanctifying, the duty also of teaching and ruling, which, however, of their very nature can be exercised only in hierarchical communion with the head and members of the college' (*Lumen Gentium* 231; canon 375). The members of the episcopal college as such have equal rights; even the Bishop of Rome has only one vote. That makes it clear that in the Roman Catholic Church episcopal collegiality is collegiality *par excellence*: all collegiality is derived from episcopal collegiality or leads to it.

Those men whom the pope 'freely selects to promote as cardinals' (canon 351.1) have mostly already been consecrated as bishops. 'Created' cardinals, they 'assist the pope' 'either through collegial action' 'or individually in the exercise of different offices'. As the organ of continuity they also have to see to the election of the next pope. It is quite in keeping with their actual significance and the power entrusted to them that the men 'created' cardinals are called 'a special college of the Holy Roman church' (canon 349). The 'more' which distinguishes the college of cardinals from the episcopal college is not, however, derived from a sacramental reference but from the dogmatic status of the papacy.

The college of cardinals certainly consists of a manageable number of members, but the episcopal college does not. This matter of numbers is a problem which certainly needs a solution if *collegium* is to remain an appropriate term and collegiality is to be given shape. That there is a need for action here has been said emphatically, time and again, on all sides, since the 1950s. The council limited itself to hints. Recently a number of attempts have been made to dismiss these warning voices as familiar anti-Romanism. But the problem cannot be dismissed as easily as that.

It would be obvious for the immense host of bishops to provide their own representatives. But episcopal consecration, which is evaluated so highly in dogmatic terms, would require this to be done by way of a delegation and not otherwise. As it has come into being and is composed, the college of cardinals cannot be this representative body. Strictly speaking, the only expressions of apostolic-episcopal collegiality so far are the council of all the bishops at a particular place – which nowadays is something that can hardly be envisaged – and 'the united action of the bishops dispersed in the world' (canon 337.2: here the legal definition already expresses the impossibility of seeing this as a group). The pope can define further possibilities (canon 337.3), but he has yet to do so.

B.   If the expression may be forgiven, the pope is the born president of the episcopal college. Any other presidency would simply not be in keeping with the nature of the Roman Catholic church. The pope would also be the predetermined president of an apostolic-episcopal representative body. At all events, this would be so large as to make a president necessary.

During the Second Vatican Council the personal prerogatives and competences of the pope were never disputed by anyone. However, there was criticism of some of the behaviour and proceedings of 'Rome', i.e. the Vatican, the Curia and its nuncios – and thus of the papacy. This is the background to the fact that a 'higher authority' insisted on prefacing the Constitution on the Church with an 'explanatory comment' which says: '*Collegium* is not understood in the *strictly juridical sense*, that is, as a group of those with equal rank who would transfer their authority to their president, but as a fixed group the structure and authority of which must be derived from revelation'. There is 'also of course no equality between the head and members of the college' 'but only an equality of relationship between the first relationship (Peter-apostles) and the second (Pope-bishops).' The relationship is to be understood 'in terms of a college or a *fixed group*'.

That the members of the college indeed have equal rights but are not of equal rank does not make the concept of collegiality disintegrated. To simple people the 'preliminary comment' quoted above was explained as describing a chain of equal links with one particularly valuable and attractive precious stone. But even then the comparison had to be extended. The precious stone also holds the catch; if this catch does not close, the chain remains a chain, but in that case the church – to keep the image – cannot wear it as a chain: its decoration is then a brooch in which the one great stone is surrounded by many smaller stones.

Taking up a statement of the council, the following became a law: 'The Roman Pontiff, in fulfilling the office of the supreme pastor of the Church, is always united in communion with the other bishops and with the universal Church; however, he has the right, according to the needs of the Church, to determine the manner, either personal or collegial, of exercising this function' (canon 333.2; cf. *Lumen Gentium* 21). Here there is a danger of Christian collegiality appearing as one of two ways of realizing an alternative structure. But being part of an alternative prevents the development of Christian collegiality. At least for the Roman Catholic Church it is inevitable that this danger will extend from above downwards.

An example of this is the oath which is now customary. The oath of loyalty given by the bishop is quite clearly addressed to 'the successor of the blessed apostle Peter in the primacy and the Vicar of Christ'. The bishop vows 'to defend the rights and authority of the papacy' and also 'the privileges of its emissaries and representatives'. He does not confess that the offices (*munera*) are conferred (*confert*) on him by consecration but that they are entrusted (*commissa*) to him; he promises to be zealously concerned to fulfil these offices 'in hierarchical community with the Vicar of Christ and the members of the episcopal college' (which is mentioned only now) (Ochoa, *Leges post CIC*, Vol. 5, col. 6440, no. 4161).

The oath valid since 1 March 1989 and the new oath of loyalty for all subordinates in the middle ranks of the church involves the making of some promises to superiors which should really have been the subject of collegial deliberation and if necessary should have led to decisions between conflicting opinions. Here the collegiality of many formal groups in the church which already exist or are to be founded is apparently not valued very highly (cf. *Materialdienst des Konfessionskundlichen Instituts* 40, 1989, 81ff.)

A survey of all the terms and images used and a comparison of their frequency shows that the 'Peter-apostles' typology runs parallel to a 'Christ-apostles' typology. The Council said: 'In the person of the bishops, then, to whom the priests render assistance, the Lord Jesus Christ, supreme high priest, is present in the midst of the faithful. Though seated at the right hand of God the Father, he is not absent from the assembly of his pontiffs; on the contrary indeed, it is above all through their signal service that he preaches the word of God to all peoples and administers without cease to the faithful the sacraments of faith' (*Lumen Gentium* 21). That applies to the local church.

But for the universal church, and always in cases of dispute, 'The bishop of the Church of Rome . . . is head of the college of bishops, the Vicar of Christ and Pastor of the universal Church on earth' (canon 331). When it comes to the whole church, to put things somewhat freely, the Lord Jesus Christ, the high priest, is thus present in the pope, alongside whom stand the bishops, in the midst of the faithful. This attitude is connected with an old antipathy to mere spiritualism, an attitude which is shaped by experience. In the transition from doctrine to life it is thought necessary that where Christ speaks should be quite tangible. But Christian collegiality can be harmed by a realism of this kind. However, it always remains a venture, undertaken on the basis of the promise of the spiritual presence of Jesus Christ (Matt. 18.20).

This spirituality is expressed in a number of ways, not least in the undertaking to keep silent. Any candidate for the priesthood is carefully instructed in the seal of the confessional; any candidate for a dignity or office in the church is instructed on the duty to keep silent and preserve the secrecy of the office. As a side-effect this also produces valuable stimuli towards collegiality, but where the obligation to silence turns into petty-minded secrecy, collegiality again suffers as a result. That was the case before the appearance of the new Code of Canon Law, when 'interested bishops had to use roundabout ways to get hold of the draft which was distributed in photocopied form throughout the world' (Winfried Aymans). There are lurking suspicions that uncollegial *faits accomplis* are being done. But here the Code of Canon Law is the framework within which the local bishops and all the senior figures on an equal standing with them must themselves become active as legislators – of course in a collegial way.

D. The Roman Curia makes as little fuss about itself as possible and always keeps just the figure of the pope in the foreground. Down to the present day it has remained a comparatively small authority. The prefects of the individual dicasters always supervise their own areas and always also have an adequate knowledge of one or two further areas. Many actions of the Curia are of a collegial kind. The nunciatures are at work worldwide, or carry out the instructions of the Curia. The Roman Curia has the privilege of being able to send visitors to any formal group of the church, which has to open everything to their inspection. The only closed body in the church is the Curia itself. That is true despite the fact that for over two decades local bishops residing in particular dicasters can be called as members. The collegiality of the individual dicasters and of the Curia as a whole has thus become more international. Beyond question the Curia has a very effective collegiality at its disposal.

By a modification of the expression 'effective collegiality', appropriately enough the collegiality of the Roman synods of bishops has been described as 'affective collegiality' (e.g. by René Laurentin). Taking up promptings from the council (cf. *Christus Dominus* 5), Pope Paul VI marked out the framework for future synods of bishops. But an agenda of 1966 already did not completely fill it out. After twenty-five years and almost ten synods, the following may be reckoned to be the most accurate description:

Synods of bishops are a 'group of bishops' or persons equivalent to them 'who have been chosen from different regions of the world and who meet . . . to foster a closer unity between the Roman Pontiff and the bishops, to assist the Roman Pontiff with their counsel in safeguarding and increasing faith and morals and in preserving and strengthening ecclesiastical discipline, and to consider questions concerning the church's activity in the world' (canon 342).

Moreover the synods of bishops take place as a symposium of representatives of all conferences of bishops and as a result – if only for a month on each occasion – act as a collegial arch which spans the world. A manageable number (at most about 150) of participants meets for a pastoral hearing and a process of learning which has both the particular home church and also the universal church in view. Through many stages – preparation at present takes two years – a wealth of agreed insights reaches Rome. Apart from an occasional 'message to the people of God' the synods of bishops do not make any decisions, which would then have to be presented collegially to the outside world. Rather, the theme discussed on each occasion sometimes later find its provisional final summary in a papal communication.

One of the intentions of the council, on the basis of which a basic law of the church (*Lex Ecclesiae fundamentalis*) was to be produced, was to revive the partriarchal structure (cf. *Lumen Gentium* 23) and also to divide the Latin church into effective patriarchates. What was intended here was not least collegiality in a multi-regional and supra-national sphere. This plan was put on ice, but that does not mean that collegiality was rejected. It was said that further experience was needed, which has now been gathered e.g. in the Council of Latin American Bishops (CELAM) and the Council of European Conferences of Bishops (CCEE).

International collegiality is desired and will be furthered in any case, for example by a German prelate being consecrated bishop of a Latin American archdiocese or by meetings of representatives of African and European conferences of bishops, or by bi-national discussions between bishops. Without European priests in Latin America or Indian priests in Germany (to mention just these instances), in a number of places pastoral care would already have collapsed. The bishops and priests in question also feel at home in foreign territory because they experience collegiality. There may be and should be many such collegial links, but they should be related to persons and tasks, or be temporary, and should not develop a momentum of their own.

The council stressed that the conferences of bishops 'in our time' are in a position 'to contribute in many and fruitful ways to the concrete realization of the collegiate spirit' (*Lumen Gentium* 23). Although they are new for many countries, in the meantime the conferences of bishops have been forming a structure which has been introduced everywhere, and life in the church without their work is now inconceivable. In an impressive way they are now making declarations and reaching agreements at a national or territorial level. The new Code of Canon Law points almost as a Leitmotiv to the capacity of conferences of bishops to encourage further developments.

However, recently a negative voice was heard from Rome when conferences of bishops attempted to speak in collegial and doctrinal terms over and above their collegial and administrative activity and on the basis of their own experiences. There have also already been synods of bishops of the third kind (cf. canon 345), when a whole conference of bishops was invited to Rome and had to go on discussing there until it accepted as the view to be presented what had previously been the conviction of just one or a few of its members.

Faithful to a wish of the council (cf. *Christus Dominus* 36), at the end of the 1960s and the beginning of the 1970s synods were held in the territory of five conferences of bishops of Central Europe. The statutes and agendas were different, but the basic characteristic was always that the conference of bishops met as a central group, and elected or nominated representatives of the clergy and church people met as a wider group, largely in the same place and at the same time.

Extensive stocktaking went on, and important decisions were made. But on particular questions only opinions might be expressed, and the decision of Rome had to be awaited, which was then followed in the majority of cases. This meant that the collegiality experienced in the synods was subsequently experienced by some participants as a special event, while others did not feel that it was really a legitimate process.

The new Code of Canon Law has similarly frustrated the collegiality of the people of God where it began to burst forth in diocesan pastoral councils. Diocesan synods – of which there were few, which took place under the bishop as the 'sole lawgiver', fared more favourably (canon 466).

The collegiality which flourishes at the parish level still makes a good impression. Leaving aside the usual human problems, at this level nine out of ten of the Christian faithful who go to church experience what is Christian collegiality. It fills parish councils, confirmation classes and other formal groups. Moreover, close communities have formed under a variety of names, the secret of which is reliable collegiality within the community and winning openness outside it. Such collegial nuclear communities often lead to a general revival in the church.

C. I would not be doing justice to the theme of this article if I did not draw attention to some dissonances which also exist. I deliberately put them at the end, but it may be said that the Roman Catholic Church lives by collegiality and is a great treasury of both technical and spiritual collegiality. No other institution on this earth produces collegiality to this extent and degree.

It is well known that numerous Catholics remain true to their church because of this characteristic and no other. They hope for a wider and still clearer development of collegiality and are convinced that only with its help will all peoples and nations, languages and cultures, mentalities and forms of religion, be integrated and remain integrated. That applies both to the local community and to the whole world. And once they go beyond a particular size, human social groups are quite ungovernable unless rule is exercised only by hierarchical directives.

Seen from this perspective, more or less collegiality amounts to nothing other than more or less catholicity.

Translated by John Bowden

II · Structures: Post-Conciliar Developments

Synods of Bishops: Neither *concilium* nor *synodus*

Fragments of a Criticism from the Perspective of the 'Synodical Movement'

Ludwig Kaufmann

These reminiscences of a journalist have to begin with a mention of the fear of publicity. In 1967, when the synod of bishops met for the first time, everything that had laboriously been brought out into the open in the course of four sessions of the council seemed to have been forgotten again. The walls of secrecy surrounding what went on in the Vatican clouds of 'broken heads' (*teste rotte*) was such a deterrent that the city press of Rome went on strike over the synod for two days. While things may subsequently have improved over the years, so that the members of the synod have been invited to give a summary of their interventions in the plenary session to the press, things have also got worse, to such a degree that even the results or preliminary results have fallen victim to official secrecy. At the most recent synod (1987), fourteen newspaper editors therefore presented a petition for better information. The overall impression since the first synod is one of non-communication. The bishops want to keep themselves to themselves.

The first step in this direction was the limitation of the role of theologians, who could not be excluded from the council, to a very few experts or special secretaries appointed by the Curia. Moreover, observers from other churches have been excluded. In 1967 Paul VI at least expressed regret that they had not been invited. Finally, there was an opportunity for this same first synod to be open for a few days to the 'Third International Congress for the Lay Apostolate' scheduled by the pope for some days of the same month of October. However, the meeting was limited to a service and a reception, and as the congress wanted to present to the synod two petitions arising from a consensus (one on mixed marriages and one on birth control), there was not even a question-and-answer session, let alone an official presentation and acceptance.

If the task of the journalist is to arouse interest in a matter, he or she is not least dependent on the expectations attached to this matter, just as these expectations are what drives history forward. Expectation initially fed on the still vivid recollection of the council as a symbol of change (which is nowadays called 'Perestroika') in an institution the monarchical constitution of which had previously been thought to be unchangeable: that it was put in question by a gathering which as such could refer to the earliest tradition (the Eastern churches, the early church, the gospel) and at the same time corresponded to modern democratic and parliamentarian views of government. The interesting question was: what will happen after the council?[1]

The authentic synodical movement[2] which the council sparked off in the first decade after its conclusion and which we journalists could share in and pass on as a process of communication at the local and regional levels of the church proved that the synodical tradition of the early church could still be realized. Indeed at the opening of the council Pope John XXIII had pointed out how history taught him that all councils, not just the great 'ecumenical' councils but also the provincial and regional councils, bore witness to the life of the church. Some bishops, like those of Hildesheim, Meissen (East Germany) and Vienna in the German speaking-area, then immediately announced a diocesan synod. In legal terms this only needed the support of the 1917 Canon Law, which in canons 356–62 and 283 prescribed that a diocesan synod should be held at least every ten years and a provincial synod at least every twenty years. In fact these regulations were a relic from 'better' times and had long since ceased to be urged. Thus in 1966 the Coadjutor Archbishop of Vienna, Franz Jachym, could also draw the negative lesson from history of what not holding synods had meant for the church's life of faith. At all events, since the foundation of the Archdiocese of Vienna in 1469 only one diocesan synod had taken place. That the 'democratic element' (Jachym) was now being renewed was evidently a result not of regulations but of the need for dialogue (among the representatives of various spheres of pastoral care and between these and the bishop) and for dialogical structures. At the same time poeple were aware that laity also had to have a say in implementing the council and taking it further; there was a reference to *Lumen Gentium* 35 (the

prophetic ministry and its *sensus fidei*) and an equal balance was achieved
between priests and laity. Beginnings were also made, in Vienna and in
Switzerland, on a very successful questioning of the grass roots: numerous
faithful took part in it or wrote their 'letter to the bishop'.

The Swiss synod of 1972–1975 was an original federalistic combination
of diocesan synods and the work of interdiocesan national experts and
negotiators. Chronologically it preceded the Dutch Pastoral Council. In
order to make it easier for laity to be included, the Netherlands church
province invented this name, whereupon Paul VI (in his letter to Cardinal
Alfrink of 23 November 1966) spoke of an 'attractive and delicate
enterprise', indeed of something 'quite new and unique'. Here the
decisions lay completely with the bishops. Nevertheless mistrust arose in
Rome: there was fear that tabus like celibacy, the ordination of women and
so on might be touched on there. In Switzerland, too, the bishops stated
that there would be 'no tabus' in the synod and the Swiss even ventured
further than others: they sent a carefully worked-out proposal for the
reform of the procedure for examining doctrine to the pope – and in so
doing learnt that the great majority of all the wishes and proposals sent to
Rome did not meet with any positive response (this was also to be found
out by the General Synod of West German dioceses in Würzburg which
was held at the same time, in 1972–75). The fact that in the Swiss case in
addition a subsequent institution resolved on by the synod – an interdiocesan pastoral council – was expressly forbidden by Rome ended the
experience of dialogue, no less positive for the bishops than for the other
members of the synod, was just as frustrating. The frustration can also be
measured by the fact that in none of the three countries mentioned – and to
this might be added the 'synodical process' in Austria[3] which was carried
through at little expense – was there a return to a plan to start a new
synodical enterprise after an interval of ten years.

So if the blossoming of the synodical movement was short-lived, during
the first decade in the regions concerned[4] it kept alive awareness and hope
that something of the spirit and praxis of the council would continue. No
wonder that the same expectation was raised by the committed circles in
the Roman synod of bishops as well, and that they were measured by it.[5]
Indeed it may conceivably be said 'in itself' that lessons for the
implementation of these synods of bishops could have been learned from
these enterprises, especially as an international (European) exchange of
experience had been carried on by the leading authorities of the synods
mentioned, in which a Roman representative (the congregation of bishops)
was also able to take part. One might have expected even more that an

efficient, historical gathering of the bishops of a whole continent, like that of Medellin 1968, which was in fact opened by the pope in person, could have been the experiental basis for the communications structure of the synod of bishops, not least because of its inductive methods of understanding the situation.

The dialogue structure of Puebla (1979)[6] could again have been a valuable impetus towards a reform of the mode of working of synods of bishops, had there been any interest on the part of the authorities that counted – specifically the pope, who was then newly elected. In reality, the modest dynamic for the development of the power of expression of this world forum of bishops, in so far any of it could be detected by us 'outsiders' in the tension of a horizon of expectation that was still in some way open, was already at an end after the 1974 synod. But on what were these expectations based that were still alive in the first decade? What structural conceptions were at odds with one another?

There was no tradition in church law for synods at a world level, nor was there any model except in the 'ecumenical' councils which we know from the history of the imperial 'Reich councils' and the mediaeval papal councils. Karl Rahner was not the first to stress that the Second Vatican Council was the first Catholic 'world council'; the point had already been made by Pope John XXIII a month before it began. Since its preparation the question had arisen how in concrete terms it could develop into a more frequent, less enormous and less expensive, and above all into a permanent yet not rigid representation of the church 'from all the ends of the earth'. The first experience of such a numerically limited representation which worked under the pope alongside the Curia was the central preparatory commission of the council, a body of about one hundred people. Moreover, with reference to this experience, on 21 February 1962 (in the fourth session of this commission)[7] Cardinal Alfrink announced the project of a *concilium in forma contracta* which since December 1959 he had been presenting as a 'crown council' (i.e. a council of chosen bishops with legislative competence). But how was this election to be made from the 'episcopal college', scattered all over the world and becoming increasingly numerous?

A first pointer at the council itself was the 'self-structuring' which the plenary of initially around 2500 and later around 2300 fathers undertook in the first General Congregation on 13 October 1962. With a view to elections to the commissions, a postponement was decided on, so that, beginning from existing groupings or groupings to be formed (national conferences of bishops and possible larger groups), lists could be drawn up and the possibility of combinations of lists could be investigated. This self-structuring developed its own dynamic alongside the official groups of the council (plenary and commissions) in a great many meetings, which were sometimes very discreet and sometime relatively open, not even excluding journalists. Here I am thinking of the meetings of the French- or English-speaking Africans, to which a variety of theologians and even council fathers like Cardinal Suenens gave lectures, helping them to develop a common view and awareness. All this contributed to the emergence from the amorphous ranks not only of distinctive individual personalities but also of an increasing number of groups. So the day could come when a council father could say in the plenary, 'I speak in the name of all the bishops of Africa'. At this moment as it were a continent was born in the sphere of the church, or, better, it had achieved a face, a voice and as such had to be taken into account.

This phenomenon of a growing continental solidarity, for which an episcopal umbrella-organization had been created first in Latin America in 1956 with the foundation of CELAM, and for which, alongside the European Symposium of Bishops (Noordwijkerhout, 1965) or Council of Bishops (since 1971) there is also an Asian federation of conferences of bishops, had a variety of influences on the institution of the synod of bishops. The continental structure became tangible in the composition of the so-called 'standing council' of the synod of bishops, for which three representatives each were chosen for four continents: Africa, the two Americas, Asia and Europe. It was then expressed on a large scale when in the permanent continental bodies there was shared preparation of the synod of bishops and at any rate an agreement about concentrating supplementary *vota*. At the most recent synods this has been learned, for example, from the Asian federations.

The 'panorama' report read out at each opening of the synods during the 1970s was also divided up by continents. It was based on a survey by the conferences of bishops of current developments and problems in the three years previous. This was expected to produce stimuli for the choice of the theme of the next synod.[8] The climax of a 'continentality', which also emerged in the focal points of the content of the *vota*, came with the statements about experiences in mission at the 1974 synod. The focal points were inculturation (Africa),[9] non-Christian religions (Asia), liberation (Latin America) and secularization (Europe and North America). At this synod, moreover, the Third World had its greatest weight, after the accent of 'liberation' had already been introduced above all by Latin

America (and especially the Peruvian episcopate) with the theme of
'Justice' in 1971, and when for the first time in 1969 both the numerical
strength of the Third World episcopate and its quite unanimous criticism
of a certain Eurocentric or 'Western' superiority had become manifest.

All this has to do with a 'horizontal' catholicity or collegiality involving
partnership, and in its encouragement by the synod of bishops I see by far
the greatest and most productive significance of this institution – however
little the legal structures may say about it. It is connected with the reality of
life and the reality of the world and takes place almost automatically; it
could be even more effective were not the remarkable idea of a consultation
for (not with) the pope, who himself neither asks questions nor gives
answers, but listens in the plenary, a determining factor both in the legal
framework and in the specific course of events.

In fact the question of the subordination of the synod to the pope and the
Curia also occupied a good deal of space in the reporting on the synod. In
practice, in all the years the issue was still what Pope Paul VI had made of
the suggestions put forward at the council, how he took them into his own
rule and reshaped them accordingly: the synod of bishops might no' grow
out of the council, might not come into being by a resolve of the council and
thus by a collegial act *par excellence*, but must one-sidedly be derived
from the *motu proprio* of the power of the papal primacy. Thus there was
neither conception nor birth, but the womb of the council was good
enough to note, in *Christus Dominus* (On the Pastoral Office of Bishops in
the Church, no. 5), that there was something *called* the synod of bishops,
though this was simply a 'council' in which 'chosen bishops' gave 'the
Supreme Pastor' 'more effective service'. More effective than what? one
might ask. More effective, perhaps, than the Curia? The context does not
satisfy our curiosity. But at all events here, without an experience, there is
the assumption of a 'should' and not an 'is'. And the one, five-line, Latin
sentence that the council squandered on the structure 'auxiliary council/
synod of bishops' goes on in the same style. In addition it can be said that
this also means, or expresses (*significat*), something 'as the representative
of the whole Catholic episcopate' – does that mean 'at the same time'? Is it
fact or theory that 'all the bishops participate in hierarchical communion in
the care of the universal church'? So here tortuous language reflects the
unsolved problem of a double function: on the one hand with a *consilium*
we have 'operative' help for the pope, and on the other hand with a synod
we have a 'significant' (symbolic?) representation of the whole episcopate.
How the symbolic function relates to the instrumental function is left open
by the text, but whereas there is a reference to *Lumen Gentium* 23 for the

former, this depends for the way in which it is exercised on what the pope 'has already defined or has still to define'. Only the note with the date of the *motu proprio*, 15 September 1965, indicates that even before the passing of the decree it was the pope who had ordained the name and form for a dreamchild of the council which previously had been seen more along the lines of a (permanent?) 'Council' (*coetus vel consilium*). In other words, the pope intervened without allowing the process of opinion-forming among the fathers to come to a clear conclusion.

This process had begun in the plenary session, in the context of the debate about the schema on bishops during the second session of the council (5–15 November 1963). The schema contained only a minimalist account of the suggestions which had already been made at the end of 1962, and the *relatio* by Bishop Carli – known in any case as being no friend of innovations – was no better. The general criticism related both to the ignoring of the 'collegiality' which was already developing as a doctrine and also the lack of inductive stress on particular needs, so that the scheme was not even any use as a catalogue of problems. The attempt to get round this by proposing a special chapter on the 'Council of Bishops' and the formation of a petitionary commission in this connection, and indeed an immediate vote, was squashed. Cardinal Lienart, who proposed this on the very first day of the debate, did not win through, although he was one of the twelve presidents of the council. Was it that procedural motions or motions on the agenda were not provided for at Vatican II, just as this right is still lacking in synods of bishops today?

Among the various *vota* for a 'council' or 'senate' of bishops, that by the Syrian Melchite Patriarch Maximus IV Saigh went the furthest. In his view, which made a great impression because of its historical and theological competence, a representative body of the patriarchate and conferences of bishops should replace the college of cardinals (originally conceived of in local Roman terms) as a true 'holy college'. Further (on the model of the permanent synod in the Eastern churches), there should be a 'Supreme Council of the Church', which stood alongside the pope and to which all the offices of the Curia were to be subordinate. The mediaeval Western tradition of the consistory was also brought out (Lercaro, Bologna); but in that first round,[10] which was also concerned with reform of the Curia, there was as yet no clarification of the various functions. Since no special sub-commission on this question was formed – though it could have worked out two alternative proposals – a petition to the pope was resolved on, and this collected 500 signatures. After the third session had passed without anything happening,[11] Paul VI surprised the plenary at the beginning of the fourth session by announcing in person what was read out the next day, on 15 September 1965, as a fixed and finished statue. The council fathers applauded because there was mention of elected representatives of the conferences of bishops, but at the same time they gave up the opportunity (which was psychologically now past) to convey further wishes or insist on those which had already been presented.

It was soon clear to the attentive reader of the *motu proprio* that the new institution brought no effective exercise of collegiality in the sense of legislative and executive co-responsibility and involvement.[12] But Paul VI saw a possible development 'on the basis of experience', while at the same time left it to the papal pleasure to give the synod the right to make a resolution on a particular theme.

In the full sense of legal validity, as at the council, so far there has not yet been such a resolution; i.e., in legal terms this has still remained a 'council' for the pope. But even as a *consilium*, the synod has only rarely arrived at a clear expression of opinion. The climax for the public in this respect was the 1971 synod: on the one hand through the document on 'Justice in the world' passed as a synod document, and on the other hand by the voting on the theme of celibacy, which was followed with interest all over the world. This was in reality a decision against the freedom of the conferences of bishops to decide on the admission of (married) *viri probati* to the priesthood. The expectation that the 1974 synod would also publish a document on evangelization was not fulfilled.

But the synod did show a degree of independence when it rejected a mixed work made up of two drafts, one conceived of inductively and the other deductively. Behind the mixed work was a jungle of obscure and complicated proceedings on the part of a variety of bodies, some of which were in turn mixed. Two things could be concluded from this: first, the double track of a 'theological (doctrinal) part' and an 'empirical part' (which was already followed over the 'question of priests' at the 1971 synod) was carried *ad absurdum*;[13] secondly, hardly anyone could any longer overlook the defective nature of the whole procedure, especially in its closing phase.

Now there had been criticism of the agenda from the beginning. Its first version of 8 December 1966 had been worked out one-sidedly by the curia (Cardinal Felici?), and after that the bishops were able to make their own insertions and suggestions at the Synod (1967). One of the problems was how the synod could be given a degree of permanency. Initially the papacy appointed merely a 'general secretary', and in essence the secretariat of the synod is still its only permanent institution. On the wishes of the (extraordinary) synod of 1969, Paul VI then allowed the election of the 'council' mentioned above at (or for) the secretariat of the synod. This election was the most autonomous action of the synod. But the council is in office only between the gatherings of the synod. It has some say on the choice of themes and also on the preparation of documents which are described as consultation papers or questionnaires (*lineamenta*) and – after the inclusion of the answers from the conferences of bishops – as *instrumentum laboris* (a working basis). It is obvious that how the questions and problems are raised is a matter of some importance, but I have been told by a member of the council who has been re-elected on several occasions that the influence of the council is small, and that when it meets, most of those involved are already prejudiced.

The greatest handicap is probably that the council cannot itself present and explain its work before each new plenary session and that it is not to give any account of it. As soon as the plenary meets, it disappears. So the synod council is not something like a 'lesser synod' for the constant advising of the pope alongside or even above the Curia. In practice it exhausts its 'co-responsibility' in the preparation for each new synod, though then above all it is the 'special secretaries' nominated on each occasion by the pope who seem to have the say. Since the abolition of the 'panorama report' (see above), despite clearly formulated proposals for reform,[14] the course has hardly changed at the synods of the second decade, between 1977 and 1987: broad statements, i.e. the reading of the *vota* of the conferences of bishops or their delegates on the theme as set out in the 'working document'; 2. summary in a number of points by the special secretariat; 3. discussion in the *circuli minores* divided by languages and the working out of 'propositions'; 4. report of the *circuli* in the plenary; 5. combination of the propositions of the *circuli* into an overall series of propositions by the special secretary(ies) with the spokesmen of the *circuli*; 6. voting on the final propositions.

As I recall, process 5 has been most subjected to criticism because it (*a*) is obscure and open to manipulation and (*b*) leads to a neutralization of what is said and proposed by the groups, so that often nothing significant is left. But the criticism sometimes already begins with the lack of freedom and/or boldness within the *circuli* and a general climate of 'censorship'. I had to note such spontaneous criticism at the 1980 synod on the 'family' over affirming or developing *Humanae Vitae*: 'There is no freedom of expression here' said a by no means insignificant bishop, who had just come from a group. Where there is such freedom and a group makes a distinctive statement, this certainly does not find its way into the final propositions. These no longer represent a challenge for the pope and Curia with which they would have to struggle.

In reality, the whole process is an empty one, which begins with the unreal and curially directed way in which the questions are raised or not raised. Therefore the name synod is misleading if it is supposed to mean that both delegate bishops and the pope and his staff are involved, in a partnership with equal rights, in finding the way to truth and forming opinion. But the body cannot perform a real advisory function either, because the procedure is hardly aimed at leading to a decision between alternatives. The malaise which repeatedly develops time and again, that the 'mountain brings forth a mouse', also has a paralysing and disillusioning effect on other bodies within the church. Unfortunately I can see no sign of the pope and the curial apparatus wanting to change anything in it.[15]

Translated by John Bowden

Notes

1. Cf. the title and subtitle of R. Laurentin, *L'enjeu du Synode. Suite du Concile*, Paris 1967. By the criterion of book production the synods of bishops met with varied interest: extensively in France but sparsely in German-speaking countries. The most important work by a German author on the first synod is the article by Johannes Neumann, 'Die Bischofssynode', *ThQ* 147, 1967, 1–27: it reports the prehistory and analyses the documentation of its establishment and its (first) agenda, but is not yet based on any experience.

2. Cf. L. Kaufmann, 'Ohne Synoden stirbt das Konzil', *Orientierung* 30, 1966, 49f. (quoting Archbishop F. Jachym); J. Neumann, *Synodales Prinzip*, Freiburg 1973, 59ff.; K. Hartelt, *Die Diözesan- und Regionalsynoden im deutschen Sprachraum nach dem Zweiten Vatikanum*, Leipzig 1979.

3. Mention should also be made of the Pastoral Synod in East Germany in which unfortunately I did not take part; it too was not open to everyone and was 'stamped by what was felt to be a remarkably antiquated "opposition" between hierarchy and "people of God"' (Neumann, *Synodales Prinzip*, 88, quoting W. Trilling). In no other synod was there so much stress on the 'binding character' of the decisions in church law and their implementation by the bishops. See *Konzil und Diaspora*, Leipzig [2]1988.

4. I have often asked myself how far the synods, at least the inter- or supra-diocesan synods, were a Northern European phenomenon: cf. L. Kaufmann, 'Il sinodo svizzero: punto d'incontro delle culture europee', *Rassegna di teologia* 17, 1976, 622–36.

5. Neumann, *Synodales Prinzip*, puts 'synod of bishops' in quotation marks, because of its lack of autonomous competence in legislation and passing judgment ranks it among the 'quasi-synodal organs', and he devotes just two brief pages to it

(47f.). He concludes that the first three gatherings (1967, 1969, 1971) 'not only largely disappointed the hopes placed in them' but also were unable to 'perform their task'.

6. What is meant is above all the learning process in the commissions, which was so stimulated by the reciprocal visits of delegates from the commissions that often a commission's own paper was edited a second time, cf. *Orientierung* 43, 1979, 45–47:46. The synod of bishops did not go anywhere near so far as to exchange the drafts for the propositions between the *circuli* so that everyone knew what everyone else was doing.

7. Cf. *Conc.Vat.* II, AP II.2, 559ff., esp. 60; the concluding *votum* by Cardinal Alfrink is in AP II/2, 572.

8. For the panorama reports see *Orientierung* 35, 1971, 206 (M. von Galli); 38, 1974, 193–6 (the context with the choice of themes) and 206ff. (troubles with the 'division of the world'); 41, 1977, 203–6, esp. 204, where we learn that not even half of all the conferences of bishops replied to the panorama survey, but that then the interventions on the theme (catechesis) produced a 'much more vivid "panorama"' (207).

9. The theme became virulent under the slogan 'Africanization' (Cardinal Malula), cf. *Orientierung* 38, 1974, 208. The hopes then aroused have yet to be fulfilled, because African bishops proved to be too dependent on Rome, e.g. on family matters; moreover an independent 'African Council' has yet to come into being (cf. the contribution by Finifini in this issue, 131–9 below).

10. The *vota* took place on 6 November 1963, *Conc.Vat.* II, AP 11/4, 479ff., esp. 480: Alfrink; ibid., 494ff., esp. 496: Schaufele etc.; ibid., 513–16, esp. 515: Hermaniuk (with a reference to *de ecclesia*); ibid., 516–21: Maximos; ibid., 618–21, esp. 619: Lercaro.

11. I.e. the first two chapters (and thus paragraph 5) were no longer subject to debate, although they had not gained a two-thirds majority. So the draft for no. 5 quoted above (*coetus vel concilium*) of 1963 remained: cf. Excursus I in the commentary on the Decree on Bishops by K. Mörsdorf, *LThK, Das II Vatikanische Konzil* II, 164 n.2.

12. AAS 57, 1965, 775–80 ('*Apostolica sollicitudo*'). As the regulations were taken over almost unchanged from CIC 1983 (chs. 342–8), and so are easily accessible, there is no need for a description (cf. also *Annuario Pontificio* 1989, 1604). The threefold form provided for – ordinary (7 so far), extraordinary (2 so far) and special synods (1 so far: the Dutch bishops) – proved surprising.

13. At the 1974 Synod ('Evangelization') the 'empirical' part had been put first. But the 'theological' part, instead of growing out of it, had already been conceived in advance, and the combination of the two inevitably failed. For a detailed account of the whole procedure see *Orientierung* 38, 1974, 228–32 ('Synod of Bishops without a Manifesto').

14. The jurist Cardinal Staffa made proposals for the revision of the proceedings and course of the synod on the basis of problems in 1974 and almost the same complaint in 1971 (*Orientierung* [n.13], 231). At the end of the 1977 Synod half an hour was allowed for the expression of desires for revision. For what happened see *Orientierung* 21, 1977, 234, and 24, 1980, 181 (*desiderata*).

15. Already on the basis of the episodes which burdened the course of the 1969 synod, J. Grootaers wrote: 'The views which the synod is to present to the pope are first censored by the pope himself. In other words, the Pontifex Maxmus is to some degree the co-redactor of the views which are presented to him . . .' Cf. the contribution by

Grootaers in G. Alberigo et al., *Kirche im Wandel*. But the most notable slap in the face delivered to the bishops in 1969 was in my view that delivered in advance by the pope. Before a synod which was to clarify the relationship between the conferences of bishops and Rome, on his own initiative he altered the status of nuncios and gave them a new role in the conferences of bishops.

Conferences of Bishops

'The Joint Formulation of a Programme for the Common Good of the Church'[1]

Peter Leisching

In the present constitutional structure of the church, conferences of bishops have found a place as a manifestation of associations of local churches, alongside church provinces, church regions and particular councils. The theological basis for them lies in the collegiality of the episcopate, which in turn has its foundation in the church as *communio*.[2] Alongside the two structural levels of the Catholic church and the particular church (cf. CIC, canon 368), the *communio* ecclesiology of Vatican II knows of a third structure with a value of its own, in the associations of particular churches, in order to mediate between unity and plurality. At this level the conference of bishops appears as a hierarchical intermediary authority with an ecclesiological foundation, which has the task of realizing the *communio ecclesiarum*.[3]

The more recent development began at Vatican II. During the period of the council, first of all the individual competences of conferences of bishops were laid down: these related to the right to the disposal of property and above all liturgical renewal. These regulations aroused the expectation that the council would give conferences of bishops general competence as an intermediary authority, with a collegial structure, between the primate and the episcopate. So some people hoped that here a foundation had been laid for the formulation of largely autonomous associations of particular churches.

In 1963 Piet Fransen saw the new regulation of the conferences of bishops as the key problem of the council and referred to H. Fesquet, who thought that the question of the competence of such conferences could become the decisive question of the council. A number of prominent theologians and canon lawyers, including Klaus Mörsdorf and Karl Rahner, argued unconditionally for the general competence of conferences of bishops. By this Mörsdorf understood competence in all questions which were important for the life of the church in the region in question, and which needed a uniform ordering for all dioceses. Rahner applied the idea of the principle of subsidiarity to circumscribe the natural competence of the conference of bishops over against the range of tasks of individual bishops.[4]

However, the council did not fulfil such hopes. The majority of the council fathers feared that a structuring of this kind would have a detrimental effect on the church as a whole. The danger of decentralization and particularism seemed to them to be too threatening to allow the conferences of bishops a general competence. Such competence was traditionally limited to particular synods, though these were allowed only a limited competence. In this connection Mörsdorf asserted that the council had 'limited the power of decision by conferences of bishops to a minimum, which simply could not be undercut'.[5] So the legal position of conferences of bishops took a substantially different form in the council documents from what had originally been conceived.

The Dogmatic Constitution on the Church, *Lumen Gentium*, which was finished in the autumn 1964, mentions conferences of bishops at the end of article 23. 'In a like fashion the episcopal conferences at the present time are in a position to contribute in many and fruitful ways to the concrete realization of the collegiate spirit.' The crucial passages then appear in articles 37 and 38, paras. 1–5, of the Decree on the Pastoral Office of Bishops in the Church, *Christus Dominus* (1965). After long discussions and numerous changes, the draft was completed in October of the same year. The council thinks it 'in the highest degree helpful' that the bishops of each country or region should meet together in an assembly (*in unum coetum*) 'so that by sharing their wisdom and experience and exchanging views they may jointly formulate a programme for the common good of the church'. Article 38 continues: 'An episcopal conference is a form of assembly (*coetus*) in which the bishops of a certain country or region exercise their pastoral office jointly (*coniunctim exercent*) in order to enhance the Church's beneficial influence on all men . . .' (para. 1); the members are laid down, the voting is regulated and the drawing up of statutes is ordered (para. 3). Paragraph 4 contains the regulation on the competence of conferences of bishops to make binding decisions; it is limited to the instances in which this conference is prescribing either general law or a special mandate which the Apostolic See has promulgated on its own initiative or at the request of the conference; this paragraph also lays down the form of voting for arriving at a decision and ordains its recognition by the Roman Curia. With the assent of the Apostolic See the bishops of several countries can form a joint conference; moreover the relations between the conferences of bishops of different countries are to be encouraged (para. 5).

These statements formed the basis for the further development in the quarter-century which has passed since then; it is therefore worth recalling them again. They were first set out by the *motu proprio Ecclesiae Sanctae* of 1966 (nos. 41, 42) and formed the basis of canons 447–459 of the 1983 Code of Canon Law. According to canon 447, as a permanent institution the conference of bishops is a grouping (*coetus*) of the bishops of a given nation or territory who jointly exercise certain pastoral functions on behalf of the Christian faithful of their territory (*pro christifidelibus eius territorii*) in accordance with the law. In content the wording corresponds to Art. 38 para. 1 of *Christus Dominus*.

Pope John-Paul II described the conferences as an instrument in accord 'with the needs of our time, effective in ensuring the necessary unity of action by the bishops'.[6]

The Second Extraordinary Synod of Bishops in 1985, which twenty years after the conclusion of the council was to take stock of the period after the council, paid particular attention to the question of conferences of bishops and their theological status. It stressed the need for them and their pastoral usefulness at the present time. Service towards unity and the responsibility of each individual bishop towards the world church and his particular church was commended to their special consideration. At the request of the synod of bishops, which had called for a comprehensive and deeper study of the theological status and the problem of the teaching authority of the episcopal conferences, the pope charged the Congregation of Bishops to work out a document on the 'theological and legal status of conferences of bishops'. This draft has been available for discussion since 1 July 1987 and numerous objections have been made to it.

This draft by the Congregation begins by describing the two terms *communio* and collegiality, a theme which we shall be investigating more closely here. In the draft the episcopal college, which, with its head, the pope of Rome, represents the external principle of visible *communio* and in which the unity of faith, the sacraments and common life is expressed under the leadership of Peter's successor and the bishops in communion with him, is firmly distinguished from the bishops assembled in episcopal conferences in the name of their pastoral concern. In the draft such assemblies are regarded as a 'non-necessary structure', which is regulated by law, but does not have those dogmatic foundations enjoyed by the structures that are divinely appointed, as is the case with the episcopal college *cum et sub Petro*.

However, canon lawyers take the well-founded position that the collegiality of bishops is not only expressed in the common action of the episcopal college of the whole church but underlies any action which arises out of the concern of a bishop for other individual churches, the leadership of which is not entrusted to him. The episcopal collegiality is given even greater external expression in any common action which several bishops undertake together in respect of several particular churches which form a unity within a church province, a nation or a wider region. Nowadays the conference of bishops appears in accordance with general church law as a legal institution, a legal subject and as such also as an authentic hierarchical and collegial authority. It is even spoken of as a 'middle authority' or a 'hierarchical intermediate authority'. As a result of this it has not lost its original character as an advisory assembly. This one institution displays two sides, as an institution with particular competence to make binding decisions, and as a forum for collegial discussion. By virtue of sacramental consecration and their membership of a hierarchical society, the 'core group' of the members of the conference belong with the head and the members of the college to the episcopal college of the whole church (canon 450.1 and 454 in conjunction with canon 336). Therefore the conference can be an 'organ' of shared episcopal responsibility in the sphere of the particular churches and beyond.

Without doubt the conferences have the significant practical task of adapting appropriately the forms and methods of the apostolate to the circumstances of a particular time and place (cf. *Christus Dominus* 38.1 and CIC, canon 447). In addition, however, Vatican II took the decisive step of allowing the bishops assembled at the episcopal conferences the possibility of 'exercising their pastoral office jointly' (*Christus Dominus* 38.1), so that 'by sharing their wisdom and experience and exchanging views they may jointly formulate a programme for the common good of the church' (*Christus Dominus* 37). For this reason the conference of bishops *qua* institution is accorded power of jurisdiction – though the content of this jurisdiction is limited. At this point we must return once again to the distinction between the episcopal college of the whole church and the conferences of bishops, a distinction which is quite rightly stressed in the draft by the Congregation of Bishops. Acts of episcopal collegiality in the strict sense are limited to the action of the episcopal college in its totality. The conference of bishops cannot be understood as an organ of the episcopal college of the whole church, nor are the bishops assembled at the conferences to be regarded as its representatives. Although there is a certain analogy between the conferences of bishops and the episcopal college of the whole church, it must be stressed that the bishops who are members of the conference of bishops exercise a regular pastoral authority over the territory of the conference in their own right, one that is grounded in this institution. So here they are not exercising over the whole church powers which they hold as members of the one episcopal college which unites all bishops. For this reason the decisions made at the conferences of bishops are neither directly nor indirectly acts of the episcopal college.

To the degree that conferences of bishops can become active as hierarchical intermediate authorities, the principle of collegiality is at work in them. In terms of their stability they can therefore be regarded as episcopal colleges of particular churches the members of which, at least in essentials, are members of the episcopal college of the whole church. Their membership of an episcopal college of a particular church arises on the one hand from this solidarity and on the other hand from their membership of the relevant association of particular churches by the delegation of the power of government through a particular church incorporated within this association.

The theological foundation of collegial action lies in the nature of the bishop's office understood in the theological sense as collegial. This form of the partial realization of collegiality in a particular sphere is characterized by the connection of the conferences of bishops to the Apostolic See and the general shared responsibility of the bishops who are members of the conferences towards the particular churches gathered together into a legal alliance.

Josef Ratzinger rightly sees the conferences of bishops as 'one of the possible variants of collegiality which experience partial realizations that in turn point to the whole'.[7] This opinion was also that of the Extraordinary Synod of Bishops in 1985.[8]

Thus episcopal collegiality is at work in any action in which the concern of bishops for other particular churches than those entrusted to them is expressed. It should be stressed once again that as members of the episcopal college, the bishops have a general responsibility towards the whole church and thus also towards any particular church of which this consists. This responsibility is specifically actualized by virtue of the close relationship between the bishops as neighbours within the territory of the conference area which is brought together as a legal unity.

Here the bishops of the conference exercise certain responsibilities of their episcopal office in a way which in terms of church law is collegial. Concern for the unity of the whole church is a central responsibility of the universal college of bishops. The same responsibility arises at the level of the association of particular churches. In the spirit of the Dogmatic Constitution of the Church, *Lumen Gentium*, through this the bishops provide the help called for, the *affectus collegialis*, the collegial disposition, to lead to a specific realization.

It is the task of the episcopal college to integrate all particular churches into the one universal church; this integration does not as a rule come about directly, but through associations of particular churches. This common commitment of the bishops in the service of a number of particular churches is served by the particular synods and to a special degree, because of their permanence, by the conference of bishops. This task of integration is the special task of the conferences of bishops. In fulfilling this task they have an authority in their own right, independent of the pastoral authority of the participants from the individual particular churches. Within its sphere of competence the conference of bishops is an institution which brings together its members as a legal unit on its own. The power of government is given to the conference as an institution by virtue of positive legal norms.

It is the basis for legal acts at a supra-diocesan level. Through positive church constitutional law the conferences of bishops are brought into the organizational structure of the church as a whole and endowed with authority. As these institutions have been given fundamental significance for the life of the church by their task of integration, their foundation in divine law is now recognized. So the conferences of bishops are *iure ecclesiastico*, but *cum fundamento in iure divino*.[9]

The association of particular churches in the conference of bishops is structured by the collegial element, since in contrast to the church province, no hierarchical bishop is supreme in its region. So within its sphere of competence the conference forms the hierarchical authority of the association of particular churches with synodal, collegial structure, the binding decisions of which are taken by the collegial collaboration of its members in accordance with the qualified majority principle. These decisions are therefore binding independently of the will of any individual.

The competence extends as far as the jurisdiction of the conference of bishops is recognized by general law or by a particular mandate of the Apostolic See (CIC, canon 455.1). The authority is the ordinary autonomous power of government (*potestas ordinaria propria*) of the college. In addition, the sphere of competence of the ordinary power of government can be further extended by delegated power through the Apostolic See.

As was observed above, the conferences of bishops are not given any legislative competence of a general kind – like particular synods which are not permanent. With respect to ordinary pastoral power there is the principle of normative competence which is accorded only to a limited degree. This limitation is shown less in the extent of the sphere of responsibilities than in respect of the significance of the competences assigned to the life of the local church.

The legislative acts of the conferences of bishops are issued in the form of general decrees (CIC, canon 455.1), which come into being through resolutions of the college in accordance with the general principle of arriving at conclusions in collegially structured legal entities (CIC, canon 115.2). To be valid, the decisions need at least two-thirds of the votes of the members of the conference with a deliberative vote (CIC, canon 455.2). In accordance with the principle of the collegial co-responsibility of the bishops for other particular churches which have not been entrusted to them, the authority of the individual bishop, over and above his personal autonomy, independently of his pastoral power in his particular church, is incorporated into the authority of the conference of bishops as a distinct episcopal authority independent of its members.

The merely advisory and co-ordinating activity at the conferences remains independent of their competence to make decisions. Here decisions can only be unanimous and do not bind the participants. These are communal episcopal acts which cannot limit the diocesan bishop's own pastoral authority.

In the exercise of the ordinary power of leadership by the conference, the *potestas iurisdictionis* is not, therefore, derived from the episcopal pastoral authority of their members. It does not consist of a sum of individual authorities. As the authority of the office of the individual diocesan bishop is related only to his own territory, even when exercised collectively and in common it is not adequate in sum for bishops to engage in acts of jurisdiction which directly concern another region than their own. Rather, the conference of bishops exercises its authority in government as a college with its own rights, as a totality to be distinguished from its members. Its collegial acts are legal acts at a supra-diocesan level. Its roots lie in an authorization which is given in accordance with general church law. By the need for the recognition of their legally binding decisions, the conferences of bishops are bound to the church as a whole through the Apostolic See (CIC, canon 455.2) – there is an analogy here to the decrees promulgated by particular councils (CIC, canon 446).

The power of decision of conferences of bishops determines the extent of the decision of the individual diocesan bishop in the particular church entrusted to him, as within its sphere of competence the decision is transferred into its area of responsibility. Here CIC, canon 455.4, rules that in all other matters the competence of the individual diocesan bishop remains undiminished and that in that case neither the conference nor its president can act in the name of all the bishops unless all the bishops have individually given their consent.

Pragmatically, it should be noted here that in practice, the majority of the degrees of the conferences consist of non-binding coordinating agreements which specifically become law only by means of diocesan legislation. Thus in fact the episcopal conference is often just an advisory and co-ordinating body. However, this fact does not alter the universal responsibility of the bishop both for the church as a whole and for the association of particular churches to which he belongs, which is grounded in ecclesiology.

For Karl Rahner, the universal responsibility of the individual bishop for the church as a whole takes concrete form to a special degree in his involvement in the care of neighbouring dioceses. For this reason, his view is that the 'idea of the conference of bishops' arises out of the nature of the church itself; it appears to him to be the absolutely necessary form of an element of the church's being. The idea of the conference of bishops precedes its concretization in church law. So the conference of bishops is 'a mediation in human law of that for which the foundation is laid in divine law'.[10]

The distinction in competence between the ordinary and the autonomous legislative jurisdiction of the diocesan bishop *iure divino* and the ordinary and autonomous power of legislation of the conference of bishops *iure mere ecclesiastico* would have to be made in accordance with the principle of subsidiarity. In Pius XII's *Mystici Corporis Christi*, the validity of this socio-ethical principle of the encyclical *Quadragesimo Anno* for the church is recognized. This natural-law principle applies 'to all levels of social life, including the life of the church, without detriment to its hierarchical structure'. Therefore the law of subsidiarity can be regarded as a principle of competence between the hierarchical levels. So the CIC reform commission logically adopted the principle in the *Principia quae Codicis Juris Canonici recognitionem dirigant*: fuller and more marked attention needs to be paid to the principle of subsidiarity in the reshaping of CIC. Karl Rahner saw the application of the idea of subsidiarity to the conference of bishops as a 'natural competence' of this conference for the groups of responsibilities which on the one hand appertain to the individual bishop who is part of the national conference of bishops, by virtue of his office and his ordinary power of jurisdiction, but which on the other hand cannot in practice be assumed by him except by agreement and in collaboration with the rest of the bishops of the same state. If the conferences of bishops are accorded only a normative competence in the sense of CIC canon 455.1, there remains the structural principle of subsidiarity which is grounded in natural law. The existence of this organ is rooted in the hierarchical constitution of the church.[11]

Translated by John Bowden

Notes

1. *Christus Dominus* 37.
2. Cf. H. J. Pottmeyer, 'Der theologische Status der Bischofskonferenz – Positionen, Klärungen und Prinzipien', in H. Müller and H. J. Pottmeyer (eds.), *Die Bischofskonferenz*, Düsseldorf 1989, 65f., 84. For the whole theme see also P. Leisching, *Die Bischofskonferenz*, Vienna and Munich 1963; id., 'Der Rechtscharakter der Bischofskonferenz', *OAKR* 16, 1965, 162–85; id., 'Die Grenzen der heiligen Gewalt. Erwägungen über die Bischofskonferenz in der kirchlichen Kodifikation von 1983', in Müller-Pottmeyer, 158–77 (see above), and the literature cited in each instance.
3. Pottmeyer, 'Theologischer Status' (n.2), 45, 81.
4. References in Leisching, 'Bischofskonferenz' (n.2), 160f.
5. K. Mörsdorf, 'Uber die Zuordnung des Kollegiätsprinzips', in *FS M. Schmaus*, Munich, Paderborn and Vienna 1967, 1445.
6. Pope John-Paul II, Address to the Chaldaean Bishops, 6 October 1980, Insegnamenti II, 2, 799; ibid., III, 2, 1657f.; ibid., VII, 2, 1108; cf. Leisching, 'Bischofskonferenz' (n.2), 162.
7. J. Ratzinger, *Das neue Volk Gottes. Zur Theologie des Konzils*, Düsseldorf 1969, 222.
8. Pottmeyer, 'Theologischer Status' (n.2), 65f.
9. W. Kasper, 'Der theologische Status der Bischofkonferenzen', *ThQ* 167, 1987, 3.
10. P. Krämer, 'Theologisch-rechtliche Begründungen der Bischofkonferenz', *ZEvK* 32, 1987, 406, cf. Pottmeyer, 'Theologische Status', 80.
11. References in Leisching, 'Bischofskonferenz' (n.2), 176f.

Patriarchal Synods in the New Eastern Code of Canon Law

Joseph Hajjar

This is the title suggested by *Concilium*. Does this representative element of collegiality in the Eastern churches constitute a test, a touchstone for the practice of collegiality throughout the church?

This is widely affirmed, but in my view with no reason. Let me explain. First, though, two preliminary remarks. The (revised) Eastern Code of Canon Law has not yet been published. However, there is confidential knowledge of the redaction which is thought to be final. Secondly, the old code was only partially and progressively promulgated, between 22 February 1949 and 2 June 1957, on matters concerning matrimonial legislation, judicial procedure, the religious, ecclesiastical property, the meaning of terms, and finally Eastern rites and the clergy. If the first three parts seem to have been received without too much public criticism, the last, concerning patriarchal and synodical structure, provoked a lively reaction in the united Greek-Melkite patriarchate, which was expressed through the vigorous and pertinent voice of Maximus IV (Sayegh) at an extraordinary synod which met at Cairo between 6 and 11 February 1958. And a patriarchal mandate, dated at Damascus on Saturday 7 March 1959, explained the reasons for this. On that date John XXIII had just succeeded Pius XII and affirmed his intention of summoning an ecumenical council and pursuing (*sic*) the publication of the unfinished code. However, this aim was never realized.

It seems superfluous to go back to the main criticisms of this first sketch of canonical codification. The development of the conciliar works of Vatican II, of a doctrinal, ecclesial and ecumenical character, made possible a revision of canon law, which has already been promulgated for the Latin Church, but is still only a project for the Eastern Catholic churches. The confidential text of the *Schema codicis canonici orientalis*, published by *Nuntia*, nos. 24–25, was sent with the approval of John-Paul II to the interested authorities by a letter dated 17 October 1986. It is presented as an organic and complete project, on the model of the Latin Code, in Latin, comprising 1561 canons under 30 titles. This is to be the future 'revised' Eastern Code of Canon Law. To what degree will this next Code have a renewing character in the ecumenical spirit of Vatican II? A rapid analysis of the canons relating to the patriarchal synod offers an opportunity to judge. I begin with a comparison with the canons of the earlier legislation published by Pius XII on 2 June 1957 in his *motu proprio* entitled *De Ritibus orientalibus – de personis pro Ecclesiis orientalibus*.

1. The patriarchal synod in the 1957 *motu proprio*

The institution of such a patriarchal synod, a hallowed term, inspired by Byzantine law, was a marked innovation, in its acceptance and its extension to all the united churches. This partriarchal synod is mentioned expressly at canon 218.1, no. 2, in connection with the patriarchal residence, and also at canons 238 (jurisdiction before papal confirmation), 248 (competence), etc. This synod is distinct from the permanent synod. The latter serves as a council providing obligatory service for the patriarch, whereas the patriarchal synod is structural, inherent to the patriarchal régime which essentially has a synodical and collegial character. For this character confers on patriarchal jurisdiction the degree of its competence and the actual legitimacy of its supra-episcopal action, in line with the ancient tradition of the first ecumenical councils and Eastern practice over a thousand years. The ecumenical councils of Nicaea (325, canon 6); of Constantinople (381, canons 2, 3, 6); of Chalcedon (451, canons 9, 17); and the topical council of Antioch (341, canon 9) are sufficient evidence of this. Some canonist historians rightly describe this patriarchal synod as *regimine*. History bears witness to the existence and activity of this specific synod both for the Byzantine patriarchate of Constantinople and for the so-called Melkite patriarchs of Antioch and Jerusalem, at least up to the council of Constantinople of 869/70 (canon 17).

Some Roman canon lawyers, curialists, assert that all this belongs to a past history which has run its course. The so-called Eastern schism of the eleventh century is said to have put it all in question. And the question arises whether the recent united patriarchates stand in a line of historical continuity and of canonical (ecumenical) legitimacy with the primatial sees envisaged by the first ecumenical councils. In fact, since the pontificate of

Pius XI and notably its two constitutions *Reversurus* (Armenians) and *Cum Ecclesiastica* (Chaldaeans), confirmed by the deliberations preceding Vatican I, Roman practice, even under Leo XII, supports the theory of the curialists. The agreements of the unionist council of Florence (1439) affirming the safeguarding of the 'rights and privileges' of the four great patriarchal sees of Constantinople, Alexandria, Antioch and Jerusalem are in practice denied and neutralized by a new principle, that of the unification and equality of all the Eastern patriarchs, without distinction, even those of heretical origin or recent creation. The legislators of the first Eastern Code of Canon Law were in fact inspired by this principle to produce a single text for all the churches, while leaving a quite insignificant and minimal space which is to serve to maintain certain special features. The 'lesser' patriarchates were thus favoured at the expense of the great, ancient, so-called apostolic, sees. The reactions of the united Greek-Melkite church were thus substantially justified. With the advent of John XXIII and the announcement of the convening of the council, great hopes seemed to have a foundation.

2. The doctrinal and ecumenical contribution of Vatican II

This council discovered and stressed the complementary importance of the local church and episcopal collegiality. It also discovered the ecumenical dimension of catholicity. The revision of canon law, both Latin and Eastern, was to be inspired by the decisions of the council. For the new Eastern Code, the achievement of the council was not just limited to the decrees on ecumenism (*Unitatis redintegratio*) and the Eastern Churches (*Orientalium Ecclesiarum*). It is important to consider other documents, notably the Dogmatic Constitution on the Church (*Lumen Gentium*) and the decree on the Pastoral Office of Bishops in the Church (*Christus Dominus*). Elements of reflection and commitment drawn from these texts are important. The Dogmatic Constitution on the Church stresses both the people of God and episcopal collegiality. In paragraph 23, a privileged place is reserved for the Eastern patriarchate, which is duly legitimated by the first ecumenical councils. There we read that 'the ancient patriarchal Churches, as mothers in the faith, gave birth to other daughter-churches', in line with the agreements reached at Florence, a council expressly cited as a point of reference. Could one fail to recognize this teaching in the revision of the Eastern code? Yet precisely that is what seems to have taken place.

In the Decree on the Office of Bishops there is mention of the synod of bishops as a council duly constituted alongside the pope, in the name of all the Catholic church. We know that this new collegial institution realizes an audacious initiative of Patriarch Maximus IV, who used the inspiration of the Byzantine permanent synod (*Endemousa*) to call for a new properly Catholic senate in this church. In this framework the decree reaffirms 'the legitimate rights of the patriarchs or other hierarchical authorities'. Now we know that patriarchal rule is unthinkable without synodal support. Later on, the decree returns to these specific primatial and synodical rights of the Eastern patriarchal statute. The issue is that of conferences of bishops. The latter would not replace the Eastern (i.e. patriarchal) synods, strictly speaking, from which they are distinct (paras. 5, 11, 36, 38).

The Decree on Ecumenism confirms this synodical doctrine of the Eastern patriarchate. First of all it mentions in a particular way these 'Patriarchal Churches, of which many glory in taking their origins from the apostles themselves' (*Unitatis Redintegratio* 14). Then it grants them the benefice of their own specific disciplinary legislation, 'sanctioned by the holy Fathers, by Synods, and even by Ecumenical Councils' (16). They have the right to 'govern themselves according to their own disciplines' (17) in the framework of essential unity, that of the common faith. This faculty even becomes an ecumenical demand. For 'perfect observance of this traditional principle – which indeed has not always been observed – is a prerequisite for any restoration of union' (16). This legitimacy, this demand, are grounded in a rediscovery due to the patristic and canonical renewal. This Eastern heritage 'belongs to the full catholic and apostolic character of the church' (17).

The Decree on the Eastern Churches goes further than these declarations. It draws explicit consequences from them which are worth recalling. First of all on 'the right and duty (of these churches) to govern themselves according to their own special disciplines' (*Orientalium Ecclesiarum* 4). And is not the status of the patriarchate one of the fundamental points? It is also good to read in this connection that 'the patriarchate as an institution has existed in the church from the earliest times, and was already recognized by the first ecumenical councils' (7). The patriarch who incarnates this is defined as follows: 'The bishop who has jurisdiction over all the bishops, metropolitans not excepted, clergy and people of his own territory or rite, according to the rules of canon law and without prejudice to the primacy of the Roman Pontiff.' And although the decree ends up in a curialist direction, affirming the equality of all the Eastern patriarchs, it declares the necessity of the rights and privileges (*sic*) of the patriarchs 'in accordance with the ancient traditions of each church and the decrees of the ecumenical councils'. And it is understood that these are the 'rights and privileges which existed in the time of union between East and West', that of the first millennium. To crown these principles, there follows a point related to the central and crucial element in my theme: 'The patriarchs with their synods (*Patriarchae cum suis synodis*) are the highest authority for all business of the patriarchate, not excepting the right of setting up new eparchies and appointing bishops of their own rite within the patriarchal territory, without prejudice to the inalienable right of the Roman Pontiff to intervene in any particular case . . .'

One cannot fail to recognize the importance of this affirmation. It relates to patriarchal synods, a specific and traditional expression, hallowed by a usage going back over more than a millennium, indicating an indissoluble reality. The Decree takes care to recall it when summing up this doctrine. The patriarchal (synodical) system is 'the traditional form of government within the Eastern churches'. The patriarch acts with *his* synod on important matters throughout his jurisdiction. Will these significant declarations of the council find an application in the revision of the Eastern Code of Canon Law? The last part of this article will allow readers to judge.

3. The definitive schema of the Eastern Code of Canon Law

Certainly the Code is still a project, although it has arrived at a state of definitive development. This schema is said to be ready for a promulgation which the pope reserves the right to decide on at an appropriate time. Now it seems to me that in terms of the theme of my analysis, a more enlightened revision is quite indispensable. I would also like to express my opinion freely, all the more so since during the preparatory work I have been left on one side, as have other colleagues, Ukrainians or others, whose competence and qualifications are clearly recognized. Among the large number of consultants whose knowledge was moderate, ordinary or simply mediocre, chosen of course for their unconditional allegiance to the Curia, some people shone as being undoubted experts. However, one could have wished that their character and their sense of ecumenical responsibility was on a par with their knowledge. Were the pressures exercised on them insurmountable or enticing to those with ambitions for a career? For one knows instances in which one or another bishop should have resisted, with a praiseworthy courage, replying to a responsible official of the Curia well known for his authoritarianism: 'Have you summoned us simply to subscribe to your decisions or to allow us to deliberate, making use of our knowledge and conscience?' This psychological factor of morality having been duly indicated, it is important to follow it with some elements of objective analysis.

This Code was conceived of in connection only with the united churches, envisaged as a single body over against the Latin church (*sic*). Is this not to mistake the ecumenical perspective of the council? It would have been extremely useful to listen to the non-Roman or non-curial position, whether by inviting Orthodox observers to the preparatory work or better by inviting them to a true collaboration, as was done in the commissions for bilateral dialogue. This lack explains the strictly Uniate character of the canons, notably those relating to the institution of the patriarchal synod. This unfortunate fact explains the language used, Latin, and the very structure of the Code, copying the Latin model, the form and formulations of which have given grounds for serious criticism.

Several observations need to be made on specific points relating to the statute on the patriarchal synod, to the degree that Vatican II expressly desired a new emphasis on synodical structure (Decree on the Office of Bishops, no.26).

We should first note that the hallowed expression 'patriarchal synod' ostensibly disappears from the scheme of the new code. We now only have the 'Synod of Bishops of the Patriarchal Church': *De Synodo Episcoporum Ecclesiae patriarcalis* (Titulus IV, caput III, can.102–112). This chapter is placed between one relating to the rights and obligations of the patriarch and one on the patriarchal curia. And it is into this curia that the permanent synod is inserted, so that it becomes a kind of accredited council of the patriarch, made up of certain bishops charged with giving a consultative or obligatory opinion in well-determined instances. Without pressing the fact that this synod is substantially stripped of its historic function, I should emphasize that it is given an organic and interior role in the patriarchal administration, forming part of its curia, while the new institution of the synod of bishops is put before the patriarch, having a distinct position and a specific authority, the aim of which would seem to be clear, namely to limit that of the patriarch.

This synod of bishops of the Eastern patriarchate is not at all comparable to that created by Paul VI, as a consultative council for the pope, gathered periodically to examine a precise theme. This synod established in the patriarchal church proves to be an intrinsic part of a see, bound to a system and in a formal, canonical, way independent of the titular figure, the patriarch. This synod in fact forms a kind of counterweight which the bishops of the patriarchal see have at their disposal, a power exercised collegially in accordance with its person, the jurisdiction which it possesses by its very function, according to all the tradition, according to the decree of the council and even according to canon 55 of the schema itself. The practical function of this synod would be to affirm the collegiality of the episcopal body of the patriarchate over against the patriarch, to guard against abuse of his authority and arbitrary elements in his administration. Certainly the patriarch is its accredited president, although this office carries with it an obligation to convene the synod and to follow its opinion in some instances which are duly specified. This synod elects its patriarch. And he has exclusively legislative power. This synod is also the supreme tribunal of the patriarch. As a legislative synod, it denotes the manner and the moment of the promulgation of laws, leaving to the patriarch, however, the faculty of this promulgation.

This synod establishes its own statutes. In these conditions, the patriarchal function, of a supra-episcopal kind, would seem in its definition, in the practice envisaged in the scheme, to be considerably diminished, to the advantage of the synod of bishops of the patriarchal church (see). The patriarch now enjoys only what we might call a honorific authority, of representation and executive office in his church. The essential reality of ecclesiastical power is devolved on the synod of bishops. This new situation breaks with a tradition which is more than a thousand years old, and with the texts and spirit of Vatican II. This is all the more the case since the permanent synod is diverted from its historic position and competence, and the patriarchal synod is formally suppressed, being replaced by the synod of bishops of the patriarchal church. The contemporary papacy would seem to be creating a new type of synod for the Eastern Catholic churches, the whole of whose competence relates to the curial authorities. This is a phenomenon of the displacement of canonical doctrine and authority, of a strictly Uniate character in the strict sense of the term. The Orthodox patriarchates could not recognize themselves in this new ecclesiastical system. The detailed listing of numerous cases in which the patriarch must necessarily obtain the agreement of this synod of bishops of his patriarchal see would be edifying. And this would show that the scheme no longer uses the significant term 'patriarchal *jurisdiction*', that of ecumenical councils, taken up by the *motu proprio* of Pius XII (canon 216.2) and again used in the Decree on the Eastern Churches (2). Instead, there is talk of patriarchal authority, a more generic term. In addition, the *motu proprio* of Pius XII had reserved a particular article for the 'patriarchal privileges' (canons 283ff.), a recollection of the agreement of the union of Florence, which expressly reserved the rights and privileges of the four major patriarchal sees. The scheme suppresses both the term and the canons, benign though they are in their actual relevance and privileges. Instead, it talks of patriarchal obligations. Canons 77–101 are devoted to the rights and obligations of the patriarch. In fact, a number of these canons indicate the limitations of faculties in favour of the synod of bishops. One cannot mention in this brief survey alll the instances in which the prior consent and opinion of the synod of bishops or the permanent synod or the two together are required for a patriarchal decision to be valid, not to mention cases in which the 'supreme ecclesiastical authority', that of the curial authorities, reserves to itself the right of decision.

The new scheme even extends the rights formerly attributed to the patriarchal synod or the permanent synod. Several canons take them up, making them more precise and extending to them the already constraining restrictions of the *motu proprio* of Pius XII. The criticisms expressed by the synod of Cairo in February 1958 would not appear to have been noted at all. And ecumenical openness or even openness towards the East is not at all extended in the works preparing for the new Eastern Code of Canon Law, especially in connection with the theme of this analysis. To the natural and theological virtue of prudence in ecclesiastical government have been added obligations of an imperative and canonical character. One might compare canon 246 of the *motu proprio* with canon 82.2 of the schema, on the pastoral visitation of the eparchies of the patriarchate. Another comparison might be between canon 248 of the *motu proprio* and canon 84 of the scheme on the role of the permanent synod. The form of these same canons, 248.1 of the *motu proprio* and 84.1 of the scheme, on the nomination of the synod and curial intervention, is just as significant. On the one hand we read this: '*Patriarca, de consensu Synodi Patriarchalis vel Episcoporum . . . gravi ex causa, valet . . .*' And on the other: '*Patriarca, gravi de causa de consensu Synodi Episcoporum e consulta Sede apostolica, potest . . .*' A clear regression has to be noted, to the disadvantage of the patriarchal synod (which is suppressed), and for the benefit of the synod of bishops (which alone is kept) and the curia (which is introduced). We have already noted this.

This new orientation, tending to diminish the person and function of the patriarch, intimately bound up with the collegial or synodical system, certainly goes back to the pontificate of Pius IX. This strategy is pursued indefatigably, against wind and tide, adapting itself with a tactical flexibility to the difficulties of the course of which the so-relevant declarations of Vatican II remarkably take account. Some who are hardly *au fait* with the tormented and long history of relations between Rome and Byzantium and Rome and the Uniate churches would be tempted to cry deceit. And in truth here we have the rigorous logic of the doctrine of the primacy, with all the canonical consequences developed since Vatican I. Canons 42–47 (*Caput I. De Romano Pontifice*) of the scheme expose the breadth of this. The pope reserves the right to intervene, even in particular instances, if he thinks this opportune. This explains the disappearance of the famous *causae majores* from the tradition, which the *motu proprio* of Pius XII had kept (canon 164). All the restrictions to patriarchal, synodical jurisdiction are an application of this.

Since the patriarchal synod no longer formally exists, its faculties of jurisdiction are divided between the intermediary authorities, subordinate authorities which still have a synodical character (the synod of bishops of the patriarchal church and the permanent synod), and the dicasters and institutions of the Vatican Curia (canon 47 of the scheme). I do not know the details of the preparatory work for the present text of the scheme. I am better informed on the studies by C. Korovelskij which prepared for the canons of Pius XII's *motu proprio* on the patriarchs (*'De Patriarchis – Studio di diritto comparato su l'odierna legislazione . . .', Codificazione canonica orientale*, ProtN 88/31, Vatican 1936). The basic question centred on the continuity and legitimacy of the united patriarchs of today as compared with the historical sees considered by the ancient ecumenical councils. Korolevskij was torn between his historical convictions and the demands of his situation in the Curia. He resolved the problem in the way described by these significant lines: 'The schema (of 1936) puts the consent of Rome as the final term; I put it as an indispensable means, but leave the *appearance* (his italics) of the decision to the Eastern council. Often the Easterners are content with appearances' (p.256).

But times have changed everywhere. In the meantime, Vatican II, I believe, has seriously sought to enter on the providential and royal way of ecumenical dialogue. And the Easterners, whether Orthodox or Uniate, no longer allow themselves to be fooled by fallacious experiences. On both sides, the shared knowledge and understanding that Christian credibility is at stake call for behaviour concerned with the truth and sincerely committed, aimed at the restoration of lost unity. The Decree on the Eastern Churches (art. 9) affirms the will of the council 'that the rights and privileges (of the patriarchate) be restored in accordance with the ancient traditions of each church and the decrees of the ecumenical councils'. Basing themselves on this declaration, the synods of the patriarchal churches of the united Greek-Melkites and the Maronites also tried to test the Roman Curia, seeking to elect bishops 'freely', i.e. outside the established list of candidates for the episcopate, in advance and in concert, with the approval of the Roman authorities. They were wasting their time.

And the restrictive prescriptions in line with Pius XII's *motu proprio* of 2 June 1957 still remain in force.

The synod of bishops which has replaced the patriarchal synod would not, I believe, be a version of the synodical reality of the Eastern Orthodox churches, which was ancient and permanent. These would not recognize their patriarchal, synodical government in the Uniate patriarchal system conceived of in Rome, even with the participation of experts and consultants in canon law thought to be well up with Eastern knowledge and desiring to give it new emphasis. For the present scheme of the revised code, as it has been established and circulated in confidence, could not, in my view, serve as a test and a model for authentic and traditional Eastern concepts and practice.

This schema has been waiting for promulgation by John Paul II since October 1986. I do not know the pontifical intentions. But for the theme of this study and perhaps for other parts of the scheme, and possibly for the whole structure and conception of such an Eastern Code of Canon Law, I would want a new version which went beyond the Uniate system, which is now out of date. Ecumenical renewal opened up by the dialogue which is already so fruitful and promising seems to call for it.

Translated by John Bowden

Considerations on the Nomination of Bishops in Current Canon Law

Pasquale Colella

1. The system provided for by the 1917 Codex

The text of the old *Codex Juris Canonici*, which brought to completion the work of ecclesial centralization in the Catholic Church while forcefully claiming the *libertas Ecclesiae* in canon 329.2, asserts: *Eos (episcopos) libere nominat Romanus Pontifex*. This provision concluded a process lasting for many centuries which already began in the time of Gratian in the twelfth century, when the founder of the science of canon law wrote that 'the election of the bishops belongs to the bishops, and consensus to the people' (Distinction 62).[1]

Therefore the normative code, while not excluding the residual possibility of elections and political influence in nominations, as a result of concessions made to states in concordats, tends to affirm strongly that the bishops, 'while being equal to the pope at a hierarchical level and in the exercise and power of ordination, and subordinate to him only at the level of exercising the power of jurisdiction, derive their power by virtue of their *missio canonica* from the pope and lose the awareness of their communitarian and collegial dimension of belonging to the *coetus episcoporum*'.[2]

In this understanding the norms of the 1917 Codex are limited to fixing the procedures to be followed in the provision of information and in the presentation of lists of candidates, excluding from any discussion the principle of free nomination (by the Roman Pontifex). In the pre-conciliar church this theological and legal approach, brought to completion after a good deal of resistance and disagreement, led to a vertical dependent relationship of the bishops on the pope to the detriment of a horizontal collegial relationship, to such a degree that it was possible to say that 'the bishops came to have a position of dependence on the pope comparable to that of the prefects on the central government in administrative ordinances of a Napoleonic kind'.[3]

2. The conciliar indications of Vatican II

The Second Vatican Council did not deal directly with the problem either in the Constitution *Lumen Gentium* or in the Decree *Christus Dominus*, but it did stress that the principle of the papal nomination of bishops should be understood restrictively, essentially as the withdrawal of this nomination from the interference by civil powers which had been noted in various ways. To this intent states are asked, whether by agreement with the Holy See, or spontaneously, to surrender those rights of presentation, of preventative consultation, of approval, and so on, given to them under concordats, in order to avoid possible restrictions on the development of the *libertas ecclesiae*. Nothing is said about how the clergy or the laity are to participate in the nomination of bishops, though it is stressed that there are no difficulties of a dogmatic kind, and it is stated in general terms that the affirmation of a charismatic church which is first of all the 'people of God' on the march to salvation, and only then an institution, and the rediscovery of the central value of the local churches, also calls for a reconsideration of this problem (which is prudently left open), while keeping in mind that 'the structural organization of the church must be realized by taking together in a single whole the human and divine elements, the historical and eschatological realities, structural law and normative law, tasks which can be carried out only by following the method of the "total" ecclesiology of Vatican II. In fact human beings, who are visible, social and normative, are only aspects of a much richer and more significant reality which comprises the newness and the specific nature of the church'.[4]

3. Post-conciliar legislation and the norm of the 1983 Codex

Post-conciliar legislation, while explicitly stating that it seeks to receive the 'desires' formulated by the Second Vatican Council, especially in the conciliar debate, does not seem to be too satisfactory. In fact both the *motu proprio Ecclesiae Sanctae* of Paul VI (6 August 1966, AAS 1966, 763ff.), the *motu proprio Sollecitudo omnium ecclesiarum*, also of Paul VI (14 June 1969, AAS 1969, 445ff.), like the Decree *Episcoporum delectum* (21 May 1972, AAS 1972, 386f.), which was issued by the *Consilium pro publicis Ecclesiae negotiis*, essentially dwell on the moment of the presentation of candidates for the episcopate and speak in particular of the rights and duties of diocesan bishops, of national and regional conferences of bishops, of papal legates, and of consultation restricted to the clergy and other faithful, stipulating that the advice and presentation of lists of candidates are not in any way binding and that all the names which remain are subject to the free and full competence of the Roman Pontiff. It also needs to be emphasized that nothing specific is said about the consultations with the clergy and laity, and that an extension can be noted to the powers of suggestion by the papal legates, which are superior both to the organs of the local church and to the will of the conferences of bishops themselves.[5]

The 1983 Code covers the problem in Book II, 'De populo Dei', at canons 375ff., and its treatment substantially confirms that of the 1917 Codex. In fact Canon 377.1 states that 'the Supreme Pontiff freely appoints bishops or confirms those who have been legitimately elected', while the following regulations dwell on the procedure for nomination, thus demonstrating how little account is taken of the principles of co-responsibility and communion emerging from the Constitution *Lumen Gentium* and the Vatican II documents generally, and above all failing to indicate concrete possibilities of overcoming the problems of the past and seeking new ways and solutions which take more account of evangelical spontaneity and Christian freedom, and also of the fact that the local church is essentially 'first and by origin a manifestation of the gospel of Christ which manifests itself as church in a particular place, an event connected with the bond of communion with the various churches and also characterized by its universal dimensions'.[6] But it needs to be considered that in the situation prevailing at present, what has been completely avoided and left unsatisfied is the demand for the direct and active participation by clergy and laity, i.e. by the people of God, in the conferring of ecclesiastical ministries and especially in the choice of the bishop, not forgetting that in the early church Pope Celestine I categorically affirmed: 'Let a bishop not be imposed upon the people whom they do not want' (*Ep*. 4.5, PL 50, 434), and that St Leo the Great admonished the faithful as follows: 'He who has to preside over all must be elected by all . . . Let a person not be ordained against the wish of the Christians and whom they have not explicitly asked for' (*Ad Anast*., PL 54, 634).[7]

4. Concluding observations

Thus it seems possible to state that the current canonical norm is quite insufficient and does not resolve the problem of a direct involvement of the people of God in the choice of bishops, nor does it succeed in bringing about a synthesis between the plenitude of the power of the pope and the awareness of the local churches. These are indeed essentially equal churches and with equal dignity, without excluding the power and duty of the pope to have a presidency which is not only honorific but also juridical, which must come about 'in love' and which must be exercised 'only by maintaining the structure of the local churches and not by destroying them'.[8] Indeed, we should note that over recent years the question of the nomination of bishops has tended more and more to reduce the competence of conferences of bishops and to increase the power of pontifical legates, as well as to reduce the electoral rights still reserved for the local churches. This certainly indicates a deficient reception of the principles of the council and a failure to apply the old canonistic principle already asserted by Gratian: *'quod omnes tangit ab omnibus trectari et approbari debet'.*[9] The elimination of all government interference in the nomination of bishops, which can also be noted in the concordats that have recently been drawn up, is certainly a positive sign which seeks increasingly to eliminate the interference of civil powers in the life of the church, but beyond question it is not enough to express the need for the communion, participation and involvement of the people of God in the life of the institutional church, in which the visible and legal structure always serves the *bonum commune omnium*, and can never restrict individual charisms. These must also be recognized in and by the ecclesial community as being authentic and responding to the divine will.

The debate on the problem over the last decade has been vigorous at various levels. Recently, groups of intellectuals (both clergy and laity) have complained that Roman centralization excludes the local churches and the faithful even at the phase of consultation, and is often carried forward in open dissension or without taking any account of the proposals formulated by the organs of the local churches, by choosing candidates either directly or above all in contradiction to all the indications of the nuncios.[10] In this connection it should be noted that this resumption of operative criteria based on secrecy which do not respect the general dictates of canon 212.3 even in the initial stages is a serious matter. There it is expressly recognized that the faithful have 'the right and even at times a duty to manifest to the sacred pastors their opinion on matters which pertain to the good of the Church, and they have a right to make their opinion known to the other Christian faithful, with due regard for the integrity of faith and morals and reverence toward their pastors'.[11]

These practices, widely disregarded, should exist and have ample possibilities of expression, especially in the nomination of bishops, so that everyone may better perform that which pertains to their own offices, taking account of the fact that in effect there are no forms of election or choice established by divine revelation. The history of the church teaches that methods of choice have been inconvenient and posed serious problems; however, the fact that dogmatic problems are not involved and that this is not a matter relating to mysteries necessary to salvation means that the criteria of evaluation are subject to the judgement of history and criticism of their validity. This is above all necessary if experiments are made with new forms like accepting a more adequate and telling participation of the clergy and the laity, especially at the stage of proposals and consultations, which also respect the rediscovery of the importance of the local churches and take account of the fact that these are not 'portions' of the universal churches, but 'sister churches united by the bond of communion'. As St Ignatius of Antioch writes in his letter to the Romans, these churches acknowledge the task of the church of Rome to 'preside over them in love'.[12]

Translated by John Bowden

Notes

1. See J. Gaudemet, 'Bishops: From Election to Nomination', *Concilium* 137, 1980, 10–15.
2. See G. Caputo, *Introduzione allo studio del diritto ecclesiastico moderno* I, *Lo jus publicum ecclesiasticum*, Padua 1987, 114f.; also F. Zanchini, *Appunti sulla costituzione della Chiesa*, Rome 1985, 7ff.; C. Cardia, *Il governo della Chiesa*, Bologna 1989, 266ff.; and further indications there.
3. This is how Caputo, *Introduzione* (n.2), 114, puts it.
4. Thus A. Longhitano, 'La Chiesa locale dal Vaticano II al Codice', in *Il codice del Vaticano II: chiesa particolare*, by various authors, Bologna 1985, 14. In general see *Vatican II: la charge pastorale des évêques*, Paris 1969 (various authors), and especially H. M. Legrand, 'Nature de l'Église particulière et rôle de l'évêque dans l'Église', ibid., 103ff.; more recently, *L'ecclesiologia del Vaticano II, dinamismi e prospettive*, ed. G. Alberigo, Bologna 1981; *Concilium* 1972.7 and 137, 1980, are also devoted to aspects of these problems.
5. Cf. H. Müller, 'De episcoporum electione iuxta Concilium Vaticanum secundum', in *Investigationes teologico-canonicae*, Rome 1978, 317ff., and H. Zapp, 'The Nomination of Bishops in accordance with Existing Law and the Draft *Liber II de Populo Dei* of 1977', *Concilium* 137, 1980, 57–62, and J. Rémy, 'The Collaboration of the People of God in the Choice and Appointment of Bishops', ibid., 67–73.
6. Cf. A Longhitano, *Chiesa locale* (n.4), 13f.; on the subject see also K. Mörsdorf, 'L'autonomia della Chiesa locale', in *La Chiesa dopo il Concilio* (many authors), Milan

1972, I, 163ff., and the editorial by P. Huizing and K. Walf in *Concilium* 137, 1980, viif.; A. M. Rouco Varela, 'Iglesia universal–Iglesia particular', in *Jus canonicum*, 1982, 221ff.; V. Mondello, *Quali Vescovi per il futuro? La dottrina dell'episcopato nella Chiesa*, Rome 1984, and also A. Longhitano, 'Le Chiese particolari', in *Il codice del Vaticano II* (n.4), 39ff., and the bibliography there.

7. Cf. H. M. Legrand, 'Theology and the Election of Bishops in the Early Church', *Concilium* (n.2), and Zanchini, *Appunti* (n.2). But see G. Feliciani, *Le basi del diritto canonico dopo il Codice del 1983*, Bologna 1984, 96ff. and the bibliography there.

8. Cf. G. Cereti, 'The Ecumenical Importance of the Laity's Contribution in the Choice of Bishops', *Concilium* 137, 1980, 48–53.

9. For the subject cf. Y. M. Congar, 'Quod omnes tangit ab omnibus tractari et appellari debent', *Revue de l'histoire de droit français et étranger*, 1958, 210ff.; O. Giacchi, 'La regola "quod omnes tangit" nel diritto canonico', in *Chiesa e Stato nell' esperienza giuridica*, Milan 1981, I, 163ff.; Zanchini, *Appunti* (n.2).

10. Cf. the declarations by the 163 French- and German-speaking scholars dated 27 January 1983, and the declarations by the 63 Italian and 62 Spanish scholars of April-May 1989, which appeared in *Il Regno Attuale* 1984. 4, 71ff.; 10, 224ff.; 12, 311ff. They were followed by further support and bitter polemic in which there was a call for 'a Catholicism which is open and above all not put under tutelage'.

11. For this last problem see J. Provost and K. Walf, 'Power in the Church', *Concilium* 197, 1987, xviif.; N. Greinacher and N. Mette, *Concilium* 198, 1988, xviif.

12. Cf. Cereti, 'Ecumenical Importance' (n.8), 51.

III · Practice: Some Case Histories

Collegiality in Action

Thomas J. Reese

The earlier articles in this collection examined collegiality from a theological and canonical perspective. In this article I will look at how collegiality is actually practised by the bishops in the United States.

American bishops exercise collegiality on at least two levels: with each other in the United States and internationally with other conferences of bishops and with the Holy See.

Because of the size of the United States and its federal structure of government, bishops act collegially with one another not only on the national level but also on the state level. Some state conferences have more bishops than many national conferences, for example, New York (31 bishops), California (28) and Texas (24). These conferences primarily deal with their state governments on church-state issues and public policy. State conferences have spoken out on capital punishment, abortion, state aid to Catholic schools, bio-ethics, sex education, civil rights, and issues of economic justice. Often a conference will have staff, including a lobbyist to represent it at the state capitol. Some have also tried to co-ordinate ecclesial policy while respecting the rights of each diocesan bishop.[1]

The success of a state conference is highly dependent on the local archbishop, who normally chairs the conference meetings. If he is good at developing consensus, much can be done. Rarely will a state conference do anything he opposes. The Texas conference has been very successful because of the collegial style of Archbishop Patrick Flores of San Antonio.

National Conference of Catholic Bishops

For collegial activity on the national level the US bishops have two conferences: the National Conference of Catholic Bishops (NCCB) and the United States Catholic Conference (USCC). The NCCB is the canonical body organized in 1966, whereas the USCC is the civil corporation whose origins go back to the National Catholic Welfare Conference (originally called the National Catholic War Council) founded in 1917.

The NCWC was formed primarily to deal with the national government on issues of church and state, government aid to Catholic schools, refugee resettlement, and social justice. It did not deal with internal church issues. When the conference was reorganized in 1966, the USCC was supposed to continue the work of the NCWC whereas the NCCB would deal with internal church issues (doctrine, liturgy, catechetics, canon law, etc.).

In fact this distinction has proved difficult to maintain. The bishops have used the NCCB to deal with social justice issues through pastoral letters, since the USCC, as a non-canonical body, cannot issue pastorals. Also, some issues, like education, have both a church dimension (catechetics) and a political dimension (government aid). A major difference between the two bodies is that USCC committees include non-episcopal members, while NCCB committees are composed solely of bishops.

When the conference was reorganized in 1966, many of the bishops felt that the conference should be more collegial, which meant that all bishops should be treated equally. At NCWC meetings, for example, the cardinals sat together at the head table facing the other bishops. The cardinals were also *ex officio* members of the administrative board. The ability of committee chairmen to be re-elected repeatedly allowed a few bishops to control certain areas of the conference for long periods of time. All this was changed. Cardinals are treated like any other bishops, and committee chairmen are elected for non-renewable three-year terms.

Episcopal equality has not been perfect. Although they have an equal vote (except on financial issues), auxiliary bishops have rarely been elected committee chairmen or played a major role in the conference. The archbishops have tended to be the movers and shakers in the conference, but their influence depends on their credibility with the other bishops. Rank does not insure power. For example, Cardinals Francis Spellman, Timothy Manning, Humberto Medeiros and John Carberry had little influence in the conference.

Recently, the role of the administrative committee of the NCCB and the administrative board of the USCC has been much debated. These elected bodies, composed of the same 51 members, have the authority to act for their conferences between meetings of the full assemblies. They prepare the agenda for conference meetings. They also must approve statements by other conference committees before they are released.

When the USCC administrative board approved without dissent a statement on AIDS, a section of the statement dealing with public education programmes with information on condoms was attacked by the cardinals of Boston and New York, who are not members of the board. A few of the board members who had voted for it (for example, Archbishop Anthony Bevilacqua and Cardinal James Hickey) later questioned it. When the full conference reviewed the matter, it let the statement stand but also agreed to write its own statement.

Individual bishops who do not get their way in the committee/board have always complained, but they are usually no more successful with the full conference. Often the agenda of the conference is so full that some decisions have to be given to the administrative committee/board. As a general principle, the bishops do not like the committee/board to break new ground. Statements that repeat or emphasize already existing conference policy in a timely manner are normally non-controversial. But new policies and programmes are best approved in a collegial fashion by the full assembly. The AIDS statement is a rare example of the board getting in trouble over a statement.

Sometimes, however, the bishops want the administrative committee/board to deal with a controversial or complex issue because it meets behind closed doors, while the conference normally meets in sessions open to the press. For example, most bishops groaned at the thought of debating condoms in front of the press and were happy to leave it to the administrative board. Likewise, the board approved a statement on the complex issue of Third World debt.

When the full conference meets, episcopal collegiality is publicly displayed. The bishops who organized the conference in 1966 attempted to follow conciliar procedures they had experienced at Vatican II. But without a pope or curia, conciliar procedures could never perfectly fit a conference. In addition, conciliar procedures would give more power to the conference president and committees than the American bishops were willing to allow. Over time, the conference moved away from conciliar procedures and towards the adoption of *Robert's Rules of Order*, the widely accepted parliamentary procedures for running meetings. The American bishops found that they could operate more collegially under *Robert's Rules of Order* than under conciliar procedures.[2]

For example, if a committee presented a document to the conference, under conciliar procedures it would be discussed, and then the committee could modify its text as it saw fit. The assembly could vote *'placet'* (yes), *'placet iuxta modum'* (yes with amendments), or *'non placet'* (no). If the committee ignored suggestions (*modi*) from the floor, they did not get into the text. This grants a great deal of power to the committees, and makes measuring the actual support for specific amendments very difficult.

Under *Robert's Rules*, once a document is submitted to the conference, it is open to amendment by any of the 300 bishops. This gives each member an equal opportunity to have an impact on the text if he can persuade his fellow bishops. In fact, the American bishops rarely adopt amendments opposed by a drafting committee. This is partly due to the confidence the bishops have in their committees. More importantly, before coming to the floor, committees anticipate amendments and modify their documents to gain wider support among the bishops.

Consensus is important to the American bishops. Although under *Robert's Rules* an amendment can be approved by a majority vote, the bishops get nervous when votes are close. If the conference is divided, the bishops will look for language that will broaden the support for the document.

The development of collegial consensus has also been helped by having major documents go through a series of drafts that are discussed and criticized by both bishops and the public. In preparing their drafts, committees are helped by conference staff and other experts. But the successful committees always remember that it is the bishops that they must ultimately please.

In their final votes on conference statements, the American bishops have in fact shown remarkable consensus. The bishops have found liturgical and canonical issues (communion-in-the-hand, general absolution, the age of confirmation) more controversial than their statements.

Of the 94 NCCB/USCC assembly statements printed in *Pastoral Letters of the United States Bishops* for 1966–1983,[3] only 19 had 10 or more bishops in opposition.[4] Of the 19, only 7 were approved with more than 30 negative votes on the final passage. Only one statement was approved by less than two-thirds of those voting: the 1974, one-sentence USCC 'Resolution Against Capital Punishment' passed 108–63. The legitimacy of this resolution was never challenged, despite the fact that conference rules require a two-thirds vote of the membership for the passage of pastoral letters, statements or resolutions.

Internationally

The US bishops attempt to act collegially with other conferences. Financial assistance, for example, is offered to Latin-American churches through the Latin-American collection. Information is shared through correspondence and through meetings with representatives of other conferences. At the invitation of the Vatican, the NCCB consulted with the French and German hierarchies when drafting its peace pastoral.

As a general rule, the US bishops will not speak to an issue in another country without making sure that what they say reflects the views of the local hierarchy. Thus the American bishops have echoed and gained publicity for the positions taken by the hierarchies in Central America, South Africa, Eastern Europe and the Middle East. The American bishops never said anything about the 'disappeared', because their offers of assistance were rejected by the Argentine hierarchy. Nor have they made a major statement on Northern Ireland, because the Irish bishops have not encouraged one.

Frequently statements are made at the request of other hierarchies. Third World bishops want the US conference to speak to the Third World debt. The Panamanian bishops wanted the US bishops to support the return of the canal to Panama. The Middle Eastern bishops and the Vatican have encouraged the conference's involvement in the Middle East. Sometimes the Americans are asked to speak out when the Vatican or local hierarchy cannot. The Vietnamese bishops and the Vatican wanted the conference to call for normalization of relations with Vietnam. Likewise, the Vatican and Eastern European hierarchies have encouraged the American statements on religious liberty. The US bishops were not eager to take on complex and controversial issues like the Panama Canal, Third World debt, and normalization of relations with Vietnam. They did so because they were asked.

In all of its actions, the US conference is very sensitive to positions taken by the Holy See. Committee documents are assured passage on the floor to the extent that they are shown to be consistent with papal positions. The last thing the American bishops want is to be portrayed by the press as being in opposition to Rome. Minutes of plenary meetings, as well as draft documents, are shared with the Vatican. When questions have been raised by Rome, documents like 'Doctrinal Responsibilities' on relations of bishops and theologians have been pulled from the agenda in order to give time for consultation with the Vatican. The pro-nuncio attends conference meetings, and twice a year the NCCB officers visit Rome to meet with the pope and Vatican officials.

Despite extensive consultation, disagreements have occurred over liturgical (the Tridentine Mass, slowness in approving liturgical translations) and canonical issues (the number of annulments, age of confirmation, use of general absolution, alienation of property). Little conflict has occurred over socio-political issues. Because of the coverage of church affairs by the secular press, the American bishops and the Vatican have found it difficult to disagree and discuss differences quietly. The result has been to paper over differences in public lest the faithful be scandalized.

The US bishops are comfortable practising collegiality. Most are proud of their conference, although they wish it involved less work. Most of the 300 members listen rather than speak at meetings, but no one can ignore their views. The most influential in the conference are team players who respect the opinions of their colleagues. Collegiality in operation is not perfect; rather, it is a self-correcting system that muddles through.

Notes

1. Elizabeth McKeown, *War and Welfare: American Catholics and World War I*, New York 1988, and 'Apologia for an American Catholicism: The Petition and Report of the National Catholic Welfare Council to Pius XI, April 25, 1922', *Church History* 43, 1974, pp. 514–28. Gerald P. Fogarty, *The Vatican and the American Hierarchy from 1870 to 1965*, Stuttgart 1982 or Wilmington, Delaware 1985, pp. 214–39.

2. Thomas J. Reese, SJ, 'Conflict and Consensus in the NCCB/USCC', in *Episcopal Conferences: Historical, Canonical, and Theological Studies*, ed. Thomas J. Reese, SJ, Washington, DC 1989, pp. 120–7.

3. Hugh J. Nolan (ed.), *Pastoral Letters of the United States Bishops*, vols. 3–4, Washington, DC 1983. Of the thirteen assembly statements Nolan is considering for inclusion in the next volume (1983–87), eight were approved unanimously. The rest were approved by a voice vote or had less than ten negative votes (Nolan correspondence to me, 19 May 1988).

4. Reese, 'Conflict and Consensus' (n.2), pp. 111–19.

The Brazilian Experience: The Brazilian Bishops' Conference as a Model of Effective Local Collegiality

Gervásio Fernandes de Queiroga

Historical milestones

On 14 October 1952 the then twenty archbishops of Brazil founded the CNBB, the Brazilian National Bishops' Conference. John-Paul II, recalling the event, stressed two aspects of it involved in the current discussion about episcopal conferences, episcopality and collegiality.[1] There is, however, another circumstance, perhaps unique, in the emergence of the CNBB: its establishment was decided and prepared, not by bishops, but by a presbyter, Fr Helder Câmara, national vice-chaplain of Brazilian Catholic Action, with the lay team of Catholic Action. When they studied the agenda of the First World Congress of the Lay Apostolate, held in Rome in 1951, they realized that the conclusions could not be implemented in Brazil, a country of vast extent and with many scattered bishops, without a body to co-ordinate and stimulate the bishops. Fr Helder Câmara made unofficial representations to Pius XII's Secretariat of State, after Mgr Montini had supported the venture. With the support of the nunciature in Brazil, Dom Helder Câmara (who was made bishop in April 1952) organized two regional meetings of bishops to win their support for the idea of the CNBB. The aim of the meetings, in Amazonia and the North-East, was to plan the church's activity in these two areas targeted by government programmes, and adapt pastoral work to the historical and social situation.

From Brazilian Catholic Action the CNBB inherited its initial organizational model, the methodology ('See – judge – act') which marked its meetings and documents, the early lay advisory bodies, and the prophetic figure of Dom Helder Câmara, at the time simultaneously national chaplain of the Catholic Action and Secretary General of the CNBB, a post he retained for the first twelve years. These beginnings and this inheritance formed the CNBB, its pastoral options and its style of action.

A further influence, and a profound one, on the structure and action of the CNBB was exerted by the Second Vatican Council, overall pastoral planning and the Brazilian political situation. The Council gave the CNBB its ecclesiology of communion and co-responsibility, at the same time as it developed the conference's sense of being the instrument for giving effect to collegiality at national level. Overall pastoral planning demanded appropriate structures. The military regime, which came to power in 1964, remained a visible presence until 1985 and still retains a supervisory role, developed its prophetic courage and provoked it to take initiatives in communion and participation.

Organization for pastoral work

The CNBB can only be understood in terms of its overall pastoral policy, its main concern from the beginning.[2] Planning as such, however, only began in 1962, with the Emergency Plan, a response to John XXIII's appeals of 1958 and 1961 to the Latin American church. In 1965 the CNBB agreed its post-conciliar Overall Pastoral Plan, which it has been implementing ever since. Starting from the national level, the process of planning spread throughout the Brazilian church and became part of its life. Overall planning acts as a unifying and energizing current in the CNBB, requiring it to have an adequate structure to coordinate and stimulate national and regional planning. It has also stimulated pastoral organization in dioceses and communities which, making possible an exchange of decisions and evaluations, while not synchronized or institutionalized, have a beneficial effect.

Along with the conciliar ecclesiology of communion and co-responsibility, the planning process, requiring as it does a constant questioning and a definition of objectives in relation to the situation to be transformed, has been a factor for unity and complementarity among ministries, both hierarchical and lay, for growing realism in choices, for adaptation and relativism in methods, and growing unity in relation to the diversity of charisms and regional differences.

Social action and the option for the poor

The CNBB has broken down the harmful division between evangelization and human development, and has always been firmly present in social affairs. Its achievement has been firmly to unite faith and life, proclamation and condemnation, eschatological salvation and the building of a world of solidarity and sharing. This has taken place gradually, in a movement from a conception of the church as outside, above and even against the world to that of the church as the servant of human beings, the leaven of the world. This process was greatly helped by the social teaching of recent popes and the teaching of Vatican II, and by the witness of a number of outstanding pastors. Medellín and Puebla, by incorporating the Brazilian pastoral experience, confirmed the CNBB's option. The military régime, by frustrating hopes for basic social reforms called for by the CNBB and by the intensifying violations of human rights, the concentration of wealth, the scandalous poverty and marginalization of the mass of the people, forced the church to emerge as almost the only space of freedom and participation, the voice of those with no voice, the defender of the persecuted, the promoter of justice and basic rights.[3] Attacks on members of the clergy, religious and lay people brought the bishops – initially hesitant and disunited – to a growing unity of action. From this period date a number of historic documents on social action.

Nevertheless it would be inaccurate to think of the CNBB as exclusively or primarily social. We need only note that only one of the six 'lines' or divisions of overall pastoral planning is designated as social action. A cursory examination of the agendas of meetings of all the bodies attached to the CNBB, or of its published documents, will show that the great majority of items have to do with ecclesial communion: the clergy, seminaries, ecclesial base communities, the family, youth, lay training, evangelization and catechesis, liturgy, ecumenism, etc. It is true that the extremely serious social situation leads to an emphasis on the dimension of liberation and that, in a process of 'circumincession' inherent in overall pastoral planning, the dimensions interweave, since there is only one, complex process of salvation.

'The Brazilian church . . . does well to present itself as a church of the poor, a church of the first beatitude . . .'[4] By the same token it is also a church of the last beautitude, misunderstood, insulted and persecuted for the cause of justice. The gospel option for the poor conditions the being and action of the Brazilian church and has created a new way of being a pastor. Many of them could talk about 'episcopal conversions' through contact with the suffering people and through attempts to be faithful to the style of Jesus, the Good Shepherd.[5]

It was no accident that it was to this episcopate that the Pope entrusted the 'important and delicate role' of '[creating] space and conditions' for the development of the theology of liberation, 'not only opportune, but also useful and necessary', which must be 'a new stage – in close connection with former ones – of the theological reflection initiated with the apostolic tradition', which fully adheres to the church's constant teaching on social matters and is 'capable of inspiring effective pastoral action in support of social justice, equity . . .'[6] Such a task, said the Pope, is a service, not just to Latin America, but also to other parts of the world.[7]

Communion with the Holy See and episcopal conferences

One of the statutory objectives of the CNBB is 'to show concern for the Universal Church through communion and collaboration with the Apostolic See and with other episcopal conferences'.[8] From the beginning a concern can be seen to draw bishops out of isolation and keep them informed about and in harmony with the Holy See. To this end, from the first month of its existence, the CNBB had uninterruptedly published its official journal, the *Comunicado Mensal*, to which, from 1970, it added the weekly bulletin *Notícias*. In both publications news and documents from the Holy See are given pride of place. The CNBB's involvement in the process of pastoral planning is the result of its obedience to John XXIII's appeals to the Latin American church. It is to the CNBB's credit that it has taken them seriously, with happy results in its pastoral work.

Dialogue and obedience have been the keynotes of this relationship with the See of Peter, a relationship which has been intense, sometimes painful, but always respectful and filial. A typical case was the episode of the 'International Days for a Society to Overcome Dominations', which sought to respond to the document of the 1971 synod of bishops on justice in the world. The CNBB's initiative was co-sponsored by the bishops' conferences of the USA, Canada and France, and supported by the conferences of West Germany, Belgium, Thailand and Cameroon, and by the leading Catholic International organizations, and over a thousand organizations and professional people from all the continents took part in it. But there were immediate complaints to the Holy See. Paul VI's Secretariat of State, after a series of discussions, declared its disapproval, not of the content, which it accepted as appropriate to the aims, but of the precedent created by one bishops' conference undertaking an international initiative, with the danger of interference in the affairs of other conferences and of loss of control by the CNBB. The CNBB cancelled the project after the publication of the first results.

From even before its foundation, in the phase of preparation, the CNBB has maintained contacts with other conferences, starting with those of France and the USA. With some, particularly in Europe and America, it has a closer relationship.

The CNBB's experience and the efforts of Dom Helder Câmara, Secretary General at the time, were crucial to the emergence of CELAM, from the First General Conference of the Bishops of Latin America, in Rio de Janeiro in 1955. Dom Helder again battled, from the beginnings of the CNBB, and so before Vatican II, to get the Latin American hierarchies to dialogue, through their representatives, with those of the USA and Canada about common problems and mutual assistance. In addition to the relationship with CELAM, not always easy because of differences in position, the CNBB maintains regular and more or less institutionalized contacts with the conferences of neighbouring countries such as Bolivia and Paraguay on social and religious matters. The conference has devoted the greatest attention to the explosive situation in Central America and Lebanon, and made many gestures of fraternal solidarity. Now it is turning more and more towards Africa, particularly Portuguese-speaking Africa, in an effort to intensify partnership in mission and pay its historic debt with that tortured continent.

Putting collegiality into practice

In their conference the Brazilian bishops unite in solidarity to face national and regional challenges which go beyond the limits of each local church and the capacity of each bishop in isolation. In it they bear together (*conferunt*) the burden of episcopacy or, as Vatican II defines it, 'jointly exercise their pastoral office' (*Christus Dominus* 38). The whole practice of the CNBB corroborates this conciliar doctrine. In it the pastors achieve the unity which is essential, without the straightjacket of an undesirable uniformity, to make organic pastoral work more effective.[9]

The CNBB has a genuinely collegial way of working, which makes it difficult for unilateral or arbitrary decisions to be taken, or for any body or post to operate in isolation. The responsibilities of each are analysed alongside those of all the others and subjected to the scrutiny of bodies which differ in composition and competence. It is not that there are no internal divisions; free to make statements and take action, the opposition, small as it is, helps to ensure balance in decisions and sets off all the more the multi-faceted unity. The fact is that the Brazilian bishops, with rare exceptions, love their conference, feel united with one another in it, abide by collegial decisions and defend the conference against attempts to discredit it or reduce its influence.

This survey shows clearly the role of the CNBB as an instrument for putting collegiality into practice, at the national and regional level. This happy experience of thirty-seven years, the fruit of the Holy Spirit and of human effort, may justly be seen as the particular gift brought by the churches of Brazil to share with their sister churches at the banquet of universal communion.

Translated by Francis McDonagh

Bibliography

S. Bernal, *CNBB – Da Igreja da Cristandade á Igreja dos pobres*, São Paulo (translation of: *La Iglesia del Brasil y el compromiso social. El paso de la Iglesia de la Cristiandad a la Iglesia de los Pobres*, Rome)

T. C. Bruneau, *The Political Transformation of the Brazilian Catholic Church*, Cambridge 1974; *The Church in Brazil: the Politics of Religion*, Austin, Texas 1982

CNBB, *Comunicado Mensal*, official publication of the conference, Brasília 1952–

G. F. de Queiroga, *Conferência Nacional dos Bispos do Brasil. Comunhão e Coresponabilidade*, São Paulo 1977

Notes

1. 'I cannot forget the virtually pioneering character of this conference. It came into being, even then with its present name of bishops' conference, . . . long before the Second Vatican Ecumencial Council gave new emphasis to the doctrine of episcopal collegiality and stressed the role of these episcopal conferences as a characteristic expression and particularly appropriate instrument of that collegiality' (John Paul II, speaking to the Brazilian bishops, Fortaleza, 10 July 1980).

2. Cf John Paul II, ibid.

3. '. . . the church which you lead, as bishops in Brazil, gives proof of being with the people, especially with the poor and suffering, the weak and neglected: to them the church offers a love neither exclusive nor excluding, but preferential. Because it does not hesitate to defend without fear the just and noble cause of human rights and to support bold reforms . . ., the church enjoys the respect and confidence of large sections of the Brazilian people', John Paul II to the Brazilian bishops on 9 April 1986, translated as *Message to the Church in Brazil*, London 1987.

4. John Paul II to the Brazilian bishops, Fortaleza, 10 July 1980.

5. 'I am referring to the image which you, bishops of Brazil, project to the whole church and the entire world, an image of poverty and simplicity, of total devotion, of closeness to your people and complete insertion into their lives and problems, an image of bishops deeply imbued with the gospel' (John Paul II, ibid.). There are similar statements in *Message to the Church in Brazil* (n.3).

6. *Message to the Church in Brazil* (n.3).

7. *Message to the Church in Brazil* (n.3).

8. *Canonical Statute of the CNBB*, art. 1 (*d*).

9. '. . . any statement by the bishops' conference produces all the more impact . . . inasmuch as it reflects the unity, as it were, the soul of episcopal collegiality, which is incarnated in a practical way in this group of bishops. See to it, my brothers, that everything is done to facilitate the operation of effective collegiality by accompanying it by affective collegiality . . .' (John Paul II to the Brazilian bishops, Fortaleza, 10 July 1980).

Episcopal Collegiality in a Wider Europe

Luc de Fleurquin

1. Europe, a continent in search of a new unity

The growth and shaping of episcopal collegiality in the new Europe cannot be considered without a clear insight into the historical changes which have marked this continent over the last months of 1989 and the first months of 1990. Europe is restoring itself, sometimes with over-bold haste, from the deep political, economic and ideological division which has characterized the whole continent since 1945. In almost all Central and Eastern European countries the freedom of the press and free expression of opinion are among the new achievements; for a number of months an increasing number of non-communists have participated in governments; attempts are being made to reform the economy; new parties are feverishly being established and free elections are beginning to take place. The unification of Germany seems a certainty, and all that has to be settled is the date; and the parliament of the Soviet Union is itself preparing a draft law which makes it possible for republics legally to secede from the Union. Europe is again, perhaps with some birth-pangs and some still unsuspected growing pains, becoming a dynamic totality of countries stretching from remote Iceland to the impressive Urals, from the cold of the North Cape to the warmth of Crete.

More than 355 million Western Europeans, around 320 million of whom live in the twelve countries of the European Community, are discovering to their great amazement that the geographical centre of this whole continent lies outside their territory, in central Poland. And more than 190 million inhabitants of the European part of the Soviet Union, including around 135 million others from Central and Eastern Europe, are again drawing on the same European roots. The challenge of this renewed spiritual unity and of a 'common home' are fascinating 680 million Europeans and in a few months have led to the impressive changes that I have already mentioned, which would have been thought impossible even a year ago. In more than thirty countries, with even more languages and a disconcerting wealth of diverse cultures, believers of all the great Christian traditions, along with those of their contemporaries who are in search of meaning, dream of a new style of living and working together, in the first place in truth and freedom. We need to reflect on the possibilities and limitations of forms of episcopal collegiality on this continent, not in a vacuum, but in the context of the breathtaking acceleration of developments in the wider Europe of today and tomorrow.

2. The Council of the European Conferences of Bishops

Doubtless under the influence of their rich experiences during the Second Vatican Council, on 18 November 1965 the bishops of thirteen European countries resolved to set up a committee to give shape to the future international collaboration of bishops in Europe. This committee of six bishops took on the responsibility of seeking possible forms of a more structural collaboration and of investigating in what pastoral areas a collegial collaboration at a European level might seem desirable. This led to two great symposia, on 'Post-conciliar diocesan structures' at Noordwijkerhout in the Netherlands in 1967, and on 'The service and life of priests' at Chur in Switzerland in 1969, in which several hundred bishops from all over Europe participated.

The real foundation of the CCEE (*Consilium Conferentiarum Episcopalium Europae*) took place in Rome on 24 March 1971. Some years later, on 10 January 1977, the Council of European Conferences of Bishops was recognized by the Congregation of Bishops. All countries, with the exception of Albania, were represented in it. Delegates from twenty-five conferences meet each year in a general assembly, which is directed by the president. He is elected, along with two vice-presidents, for a term of three years. A general secretariat based in Chur, Switzerland, is responsible for administrative support. It is remarkable that years before the pontificate of John Paul II began and the first signs of new life were visible in Central and Eastern Europe, conferences of bishops throughout the continent were involved. At this level episcopal collegiality preceded the subsequent social changes. But it is only recently that the first bishops from Lithuania, Romania and Czechoslovakia have actually been able to take part in activities.

The Council itself does not have juridical competence over the conferences of bishops which provide its members or over their particular churches. The main responsibilities envisaged in its statutes are encouraging reciprocal contacts, working out pastoral initiatives together and organizing study days and symposia.

Between October 1975 and October 1989 five new symposia took place in Rome in which sometimes more than a hundred bishops and advisors participated. A limited number of representatives of European associations for priests, laity, superiors of religious orders and the federation of Catholic international organizations were also invited to these symposia. During the last symposium, which was held between 9 and 13 October 1989, an attempt was made to arrive at a Christian attitude to the contemporary experience of birth and death in a strongly secularized Europe. The far-reaching individualization of human existence today and the lack of opportunities to come to terms with one's own suffering and death stress the need for such a symposium.

The numerous non-statutory and unofficial meetings are extremely important for real episcopal collegiality. These offer important opportunities for widening horizons and lead to the discovery of the same or of very different problems in the various countries. Common solutions in the former case or much more understanding of the unique situation of well-defined particular churches in the latter beyond doubt encourage a better and sometimes very complex rooting of Christianity in each culture. Historical tensions between neighbouring countries can also be revitalized and already existing contacts be expanded. In assessing the unmistakable growing collaboration between bishops at a European level one may certainly not lose sight of the psychological attitudes of particular peoples to one another, the tendency towards isolation from other countries, and sometimes even certain feelings of superiority on the part of individuals or countries. Therefore all these varied forms of collaboration call for much patience and the time which is needed for maturity and growth.

The lack of a common language which is spoken or known well throughout the continent does not make the organization of collegial collaboration easy. Delegates from the wider language-areas often have little linguistic knowledge outside their mother tongue. In smaller informal groups the composition of the group determines which languages are spoken. In many cases this leads to the use of French and German, though younger generations of bishops increasingly speak in English. During the symposia French, German, English, Italian and to a certain degree Spanish are used. In many cases, particularly in Belgium, Switzerland and Czechoslovakia, the different conferences of bishops are themselves already multi-lingual. The small Scandinavian conference of bishops includes bishops from five different countries, speaking that many different languages. Whatever irreplaceable wealth the multiplicity of cultures and languages may represent for the European continent, this remains a practical difficulty at international meetings which must not be underestimated. At present, serious efforts are being made at universities throughout Europe to encourage the learning of foreign languages. The target is worth the trouble, namely that in addition to their mother tongue or the languages spoken in their country all students should have a sufficient command of English and one other foreign language, preferably that of a neighbouring country. If episcopal collegiality which extends beyond frontiers is to be achieved, great importance must be attached to adequate linguistic knowledge.

Despite the problem of language and other obstacles to organization, European bishops meet one another in an increasing variety of meetings. Members of the conferences of bishops responsible for particular pastoral sectors meet one another on formal and informal study days, which make it possible to compare notes over experiences and to exchange information and projects. Hitherto this has applied to bishops who were particularly burdened with responsibility for communication in the media, catechesis, tourism, migrants, pastoral work among youth, pilgrimage orders, ecumenism, the mission of the laity, and finally the protection of human rights, peace and justice.

In addition to a series of meetings of the presidents of the conferences of bishops in Europe, two new more recent initiatives of episcopal collegiality may be mentioned. On several occasions already a meeting has been organized of the diocesan bishops of about fifteen major European cities: London, Madrid, Berlin, Cologne, Munich, Paris, Brussels, Naples, Warsaw, Vienna and so on. The organization of pastoral work in the great cities in various areas and for specific groups of people involves particularly complicated problems, and information from all these different cities is an important contribution to the search for a common view and common solutions. The most recent meeting, under the heading 'The Bishop's Mission in Contemporary Europe', was held during the second half of January 1990.

A second particularly interesting initiative is the training of newly appointed bishops. In 1988 there were around a hundred diocesan bishops in Europe who had not yet had five years' experience in leading their dioceses. They were invited for a session in which the bishop's task of proclamation and his personal spiritual life were the subject of special discussion. About thirty bishops enrolled for the session; at all events, this indicates the need for this kind of activity. For the sake of completeness it should be mentioned that this last initiative came from the Council of European Conferences of Bishops, while the meeting of the bishops of great European cities must be regarded as an informal expression of collegiality.

As I already mentioned in the introduction, one of the characteristics of European culture is that all the great families of Christendom have strong roots and many tens of millions of faithful in the same continent. In some countries the Roman Catholic church is very strong or is almost the only church. This is the case, for example, in Portugal, Spain, Italy, Ireland, Austria, Luxembourg and Belgium. In other countries Catholic believers are very much in the minority or amount to around half the population. The Netherlands, the German Federal Republic, Czechoslovakia, Hungary and Switzerland are good examples of this. By contrast, a traditionally deep rooting of the Orthodox, Anglican or Lutheran churches in other European countries means that the number of Catholics is quite limited. Sometimes they number less than one per cent of the total population. Denmark, Greece, Norway and Finland may be mentioned in this connection. No one should be surprised that a good deal of attention is paid to ecumenical activities by European bishops, though to differing degrees, because of the very different religious situations in their own countries which have grown up over history.

In collaboration with the Conference of European Churches (KEK) which has existed since 1959, in 1978, 1981, 1984 and 1988 the Council of European Conferences of Bishops organized large ecumenical meetings in which forty representatives from the Catholic side and forty representatives from the KEK met together in prayer, study and dialogue. In addition, since 1971 there has also been a joint committee which meets annually. The great ecumenical meeting in Basel, Switzerland, from 15 to 21 May 1989, would have been impossible without intense ecumenical contacts lasting over years. Some see the intense ecumenical dialogue in many places in Europe as an unexpected consequence of the establishment of conferences of bishops at a national level and of the international collaboration which they subsequently brought. Perhaps Europe, which is largely responsible for deep religious splits in Christendom, is also increasingly engaged in bridging them over.

3. The Commission of Episcopates of the European Community

This form of collegial collaboration of European bishops developed because of a very specific need in the late 1970s. The establishment of the COM.E.C.E (*Commissio Episcopatuum Communitatis Europaeae*) in 1980 did not come about with direct pastoral ends in view but in order to further relations between the bishops of the twelve countries of the European Community and the central European Community institutions. The thirteen conferences of bishops, including one English and one Scottish, each sent a bishop as delegate to the annual General Assembly. The Swiss and Austrian conferences were invited as observers. Through the person of the Secretary General close contact is maintained with the EEC and the nuncio to the European Community. However, there is not room in such a brief contribution to discuss in detail the working of this less well-known but nevertheless important institution.

4. Conclusion

The collegial collaboration of bishops in Europe has brought out the bewildering complexity of church life in this continent particularly clearly. However, a strong desire for far more formal and above all informal meetings within the church and also ecumenically indicates an intense concern to make dynamic progress. Both better communication of information to the dioceses and a more developed infrastructure could make an important contribution here. For the ultimate aim of all episcopal collegiality involves bishops in standing alongside their contemporaries in order to live in truth and freedom as authentic believers in the new Europe.

Translated by John Bowden

Dialogue of Life: The Experience of the Federation of Asian Bishops' Conferences

Julio X. Labayen

1. The Asian situation

Asia defies generalization. It is a continent of ancient and diverse cultures, religions, histories and traditions. It is also a continent of the young: nearly sixty per cent of its people are below twenty-five years of age. Two-thirds of humankind lives in Asia. It is a population largely marked with poverty, undernourishment, ill-health, scarred by war and suffering, troubled and restless. It is a continent of awakened masses with a new consciousness and a new self-understanding of their subjugation by foreign domination, who now aspire to a better and fuller life.

This was the situation in Asia when the Asian bishops met for the first time in Manila on November 1970. Pope Paul VI presided at this Asian bishops' meeting.

The Asian bishops chose *development* as the theme of their meeting, coupled with their concern for the *young*, who were then marching in the streets crying for freedom and democracy.

2. The FABC – Its conception and birth

It was in the spirit of *collegiality* and *dialogue* that the Asian bishops met. Their objective was to discover new ways through which they may be of greater and more effective service to their communities, to the peoples of Asia, and to the future, pregnant with both fear and promise (Message of the Conference no. 2).

With this in mind the Asian bishops resolved to put up an effective instrument that would implement the resolutions of the meeting. They agreed 'that the episcopal conferences here represented are urged to authorize and support a permanent structure for the effective implementation of the decisions of this meeting'. A follow-up committee was formed to set up this structure and to request the Holy See for its approval. Pope Paul VI approved the Statutes of the Federation of Asian Bishops' Conferences (FABC) on 16 November 1972.

Respecting the desire of the episcopal conferences, the FABC statutes provide for a federation that would foster collegiality and dialogue, and respect and uphold the autonomy of the different episcopal conferences.

3. The structure

The FABC comprises the episcopal conferences of the following countries: India, Pakistan, Bangladesh, Sri Lanka, Burma, Laos-Cambodia, Vietnam, Thailand, Indonesia, Philippines, Taiwan, Korea, Japan; also Hong Kong and Macao.

The following is the set-up of the FABC:

1. A *central committee* which consists of the president of each episcopal conference or his episcopal representative. The function of this body is to foster and coordinate the efforts of the episcopal conferences to implement the resolutions of the FABC.

2. A *standing committee* of three bishops appointed by the central committee.

3. A *central secretariat*, headed by a secretary general, who is appointed by the central committee. This secretariat functions under the guidance of the standing committee. Its functions are to promote continuing cooperation among the episcopal conferences of Asia, to be an organ of exchange of information, to be a centre which sets up consultations, conferences and the like, to serve as a channel of dissemination of thought on social questions, to study the possibilities of mutual aid between the Catholic communities in Asia and between the Catholic communities of the West and those of Asia, to promote formation of a common mind and a common voice on questions of justice, development and peace, to serve as liaison with the Christian Conference of Asia, and to serve as liaison between the Christians of Asia and their brethren of other faiths.

4. *Offices* constituted by the central committee which are responsible for the areas indicated by the FABC. These areas are: human development, social communications, education and student chaplaincy, evangelization, ecumenical and inter-religious affairs. After the bishops' synod of 1986 a committee for the laity was set up (Annex 4, Resolution on Structure, ABM, FABC Papers, no. 28).

4. The life of the FABC: plenary assembly and institutes

To be of better and more effective service to their peoples, the Asian bishops in their first plenary assembly resolved to promote a *dialogue of life*. 'It involves a genuine experience and understanding of . . . poverty, deprivation and oppression of . . . our peoples. It demands working, not for them merely . . . . but *with* them to learn from them . . . their real needs and aspirations, as they are enabled to identify and articulate them, and to strive for their fulfilment, by transforming those structures and situations which keep them in that deprivation and powerlessness' (no. 20).

The plenary assemblies sustain and promote the life of the FABC. They take place every four years. Their themes are determined by the vital interests in Asia and the concerns of the Bishops' Synod. They are: 1. Evangelization in Modern-Day Asia (1974); 2. Prayer – The Life of the Church in Asia (1978); 3. The Church – A Community of Faith in Asia (1982); 4. The Vocation and Mission of the Laity in the Church and in the World of Asia (1986).

Moreover, and perhaps more effectively, the dialogue of life is nourished and deepened by the methodology which has been adopted by the various offices in their institutes. It is called exposure/immersion. It starts with an experiential sharing of the life of our poor people in their hovels, their place of work and worship. The data of this experience is submitted to a social analysis to discover the forces at work in their lives, forces *for* or *against* their deepest aspirations. This analysis is further subjected to theological reflection in order to read the signs in the light of the gospel. Finally, a response is solicited from the bishops, in terms of how best they can serve their people as pastors and bearers of the good news of God's kingdom.

5. Ten years of FABC: an evaluation

The third plenary assembly (1982) which marked the tenth anniversary of the FABC evaluated what the FABC has done for the episcopal conferences, and how these have been inadequate in their response.

Briefly, the assembly recounts what the FABC has done for its constituency:

1. The Asian bishops have come to know and understand one another better, and bonds of friendship and solidarity have grown among them. There is better appreciation of each other's episcopal conference and local churches, and a sharing in common of joys, setbacks, sorrows and griefs.

2. We . . . have been taught to pray with and for each other; to learn

from one another; to share common pastoral and theological concerns; to be reached by great ecclesial initiatives and movements; to work together and to share our material and personnel resources – in brief, to become truly sister churches . . .

3. The several offices of the FABC, with their institutes, seminars and formation courses, have taught us to reflect together on the situations which exist in our countries, on the needs of our peoples, and how we might more effectively respond to them.

4. We have also been enabled . . . to contribute to the on-going reflection and discernment of churches in other continents and to the thinking and policies of the central administration of the church.

5. As our mutual knowledge, affection and esteem have grown for each other, so has our gratitude for the unity that is the Lord's gift to us. We have learned to understand the role of the See of Peter, and we have felt keenly in our meetings the absence of our brother bishops from the churches in those countries which have not permitted their participation.

6. The last ten years have not been without significance for the realization of our hope which we expressed in our historic meeting in Manila in 1970, that the Church in Asia may in some small way become a sacrament . . . of the unity of our peoples.

7. Our plenary assemblies manifest our concerns: (a) our churches' mission and service to our Asian peoples; (b) their life of prayer, in the interiority of persons and in the inner life of our communities, and the bonds that link our Christian prayer with the prayer and spirituality of other religious traditions in Asia; (c) the ministries in local churches in their respective contexts.

In the same manner the assembly humbly admits how the bishops have fallen short. Here are some of these inadequacies and failures:

1. In our inner convictions and personal and collective spirituality there has often been insufficient interiorization of, and conversion to, the teaching of the gospel and the council on authentic Christian community.

2. In our . . . living with each other we have inadequately manifested true communion and participation: all too often perhaps in the exercise of authority there still persists a spirit of domination, instead of the reality of Christlike servanthood; in the presbyteral communities and religious houses often true co-responsibility is not manifest; in our parish and diocesan communities not rarely the evident realization . . . of love is not to be found.

3. The structures of our ecclesial organization often image forth 'institution' in its less attractive aspects, and not 'community'; church

groups not infrequently remain individualist in ethos and practice. Sometimes organs of lay participation and co-responsibility have not been established, or are left inactive and impeded . . . Often enough the gifts and charisms of the laity, both men and women, are not duly recognized, welcomed or activated in significant functions and tasks of ministry and apostolate.

4. In many cases adequate formation in the authentic ecclesiology of Vatican II has not yet been provided.

5. Although . . . much progress has been made in formation to, and exercise of, prayer, still much remains to be done toward fostering it in our communities.

6. How often too our communities, in relation to the communities of other faiths . . . have failed to be communities of dialogue.

7. How often too, our communities, especially among those more favored in life, have failed to grow in awareness of situations of social injustice, of the violation of human dignity and human rights massively present among them.

8. How little . . . have we spoken or taken action against the oppression and degradation of women, especially among the poor and less educated, for the purpose and profit of various exploitative industries, tourism and sex-trades.

9. Finally, how often insufficient for the most part has been our missionary consciousness and responsibility.

6. Conclusion

To conclude, the Federation has indeed made us realize our responsibility as pastors among our peoples. It has opened our minds and hearts to the realities of our peoples in Asia, particularly their massive deprivation and impoverishment on one hand, and their rich religio-cultural heritage on the other. It has likewise promoted for us a true sense of *collegiality* in communion with the successor of Peter and with our brother bishops in Asia and in other continents, a communion that we feel must be reflected in our dioceses and Christian communities, not only *ad intra* but also *ad extra* in our relationship with communities of other faiths. Above all, the *dialogue of life* which we strive to live up to has deepened our understanding of what it means to be the *Catholic* church in modern Asia and of the reason why we are sent to this vast continent which is the cradle of the great world religions.

For all these graces we give thanks. For all our shortcomings and failures we ask forgiveness.

Episcopal Collegiality: Reflections on African Experience

Antoine Matenkadi Finifini

This is not the place for making an in-depth analysis of the expression 'episcopal collegiality'. The topic is both complicated and wide-ranging. So I shall limit myself to developing two lines here. First I shall report on the forms of episcopal collegiality which have in fact been achieved in Africa. Then I shall offer a series of reflections on the future of episcopal collegiality on that continent.

1. Notions of episcopal collegiality

The ecclesial communion which derives its profound reality from the unity of the Father, the Son and the Holy Spirit is expressed in the unity of the episcopal college, the unity of the bishops among themselves and their unity with Peter's successor, under his authority (*Lumen Gentium* 22; CIC, canon 336). The theological and canonical language which denotes this visible and external form of the unity of the church makes use of the term 'episcopal collegiality'.[1] The episcopal college exercises power over the whole church in a solemn manner in the ecumenical council (CIC, canon 337.1). The ecumenical council, which occupies a privileged place in the life of the church, is the most evident form of the exercising of episcopal collegiality.

The doctrine of episcopal collegiality recognizes not only the universal exercising of this collegiality throughout the church, as in the ecumenical council, for example, but also a more limited exercising of it within a region. To reduce the theme of collegiality to the relationship between the members and the pope, their head, would be inadequate. Collegiality also appears in the mutual relationship of members of the college among themselves.

So at a more modest level, in different ways there are varied formulae and modalities which relate to episcopal collegiality. Among the ways in which episcopal collegiality is exercised at a regional level we shall come across particular councils, conferences of bishops and regroupings of conferences of bishops.

2. African experience

A. *Effective collegiality*

An examination of the forms of episcopal collegiality effectively realized on the African continent will note first of all the conferences of bishops, the regional regrouping of conferences of bishops and the symposium of the Episcopal Conferences of Africa and Madagascar (SCEAM) at the continental level.

(a)   Conferences of bishops

The conferences of bishops, which are useful and indispensable into the present organization of pastoral work, correspond to the territorial exercise of episcopal collegiality. From a strictly theological point of view, Vatican II mentions that the episcopal conferences contribute in many fruitful ways to the concrete realization of collegial feeling (*Lumen Gentium* 23). Conferences of bishops as an episcopal body only have substance and reality in hierarchical communion with the Bishop of Rome.

The importance of conferences of bishops in Africa is so clear that there is no need to spend too much time on it. The active participation of numerous delegates of these conferences of bishops at the different synods of bishops is eloquent proof of their vitality and their communion with the whole church. The 1988 *Pontifical Annuary* mentions the existence of thirty-one conferences of bishops in Africa.

(b)   Associations of conferences of bishops

This episcopal collegiality is also exercised through associations of conferences of bishops which are coming into being on the African continent. There are now seven of these. AMECEA (Association of Member Episcopal Conferences of Eastern Africa) is the oldest regional episcopal association on the continent; the association was born at a first meeting held in Dar-es-Salaam in 1961. Others are the Inter-Regional Meeting of Bishops of Southern Africa (IMBiSA), the Association of the Episcopal Conferences of Anglophone West Africa (AECAWA), the Regional Episcopal Conference of Francophone West Africa (CERAO), the Regional Episcopal Conference of North Africa (CERNA), the Association of Episcopal Conferences of the Region of Central Africa (ACERAC) and the Association of Episcopal Conferences of Central Africa (ACEAC), of which Zaire is a member.

(c) SCEAM

At a continental level, the church of Africa has an organization which brings together all the conferences of bishops of Africa and Madagascar. It is called the Symposium of Episcopal Conferences of Africa and Madagascar (SCEAM); its creation at Kampala[2] in 1969 coincided with the first visit of a pope to Africa, in the person of Pope Paul VI.

Collegiality, a concept given new dynamism by Vatican II and rapidly implemented, proved to be the motivating principle in the constitution of an organism which made the church in Africa capable of making its own voice heard within the universal church. Justifying the need for an organism of the episcopate which covered all Africa and Madagascar, Cardinal Zoungrana said that a pan-African organism of the episcopate would carry special weight in alerting the opinion of the church 'in season and out of season' to its responsibilities in Africa and Madagascar.[3] SCEAM is the manifestation of a common mind of the bishops on the subject of the life of the church in Africa.

Conceived of by the bishops before the Vatican II sessions, among others things because of the fragmentary character of the African episcopate, SCEAM is the fruit of the collegial solidarity which Africa experienced at the Second Vatican Council. It is certainly the case, as Cardinal Zoungrana pointed out, that during the council the bishops of Africa stood out as giving an example of spontaneously united group in a pan-African episcopal conference.

B. Expectations

Alongside forms of episcopal collegiality which have in fact been realized, there are other forms of collegiality which are not yet celebrated, like particular councils and the 'African Council', or are in process of realization, like the special synod for Africa.

(a) Particular councils

The 1983 Code of Canon Law mentions two kinds of particular councils, plenary and provincial councils (canons 439–446). One brings together all the bishops of the same nation or territory which has a single conference of bishops (canon 439). The other brings together all the bishops of the same church province (canon 440). Each has 'legislative power so that with due regard always for the universal law of the Church it can decree what seems appropriate for increasing faith, organizing common pastoral activity, directing morals and preserving, promoting or protecting common ecclesiastical discipline' (canon 445). Decrees of these councils have the force of law only after being recognized by the Holy See. Moreover, the approval of the Apostolic See is required to convene a plenary council.

(b)   Council and synod in Africa

Particular councils remain the canonical and ecclesial gatherings that the particular churches of the African content have not so far celebrated. However, on 6 January 1989, the Feast of the Epiphany, Pope John-Paul II took a decision in favour of an ecclesial event proper to Africa: in response, he said, to the request often made for some time by the Africans.[5] He has decided to convoke a special assembly of the synod of bishops for Africa on the theme 'Churches of Africa at the Dawn of the Third Milennium'.

Why a synod, when the voices which have been raised in Africa have explicitly expressed the desire for an 'African council'?[6]

The expression 'African council', which emerged in public at the colloquy on 'Black Civilization and the Catholic Church', held at Abidjan on the Ivory Coast in 1977 at the prompting of the lay Catholic Alioune Diop, made its way through two continental African authorities, the special mission of some African theologians who went to make contact with the European Christian public,[7] the first pastoral visit of John-Paul II to Zaire and the *ad limina* visit of the bishops of Zaire in 1983.

In fact, on 12 April 1983, through Cardinal Malula, its spokesman, the episcopate of Zaire repeated the desire already expressed in 1980 to see the celebration one day of an African council which 'will allow our churches to sum up the situation of Christianity in Africa and to establish together adequate foundations for the integral evangelization of our continent in the future'. In his allocution in response to the bishops of the second group of the Zaire episcopat, Mgr Tschibangu writes, on 21 April 1983 Pope John-Paul expressed his agreement to the project in principle in the following terms: '. . . to respond to a desire which you have expressed concerning the whole church in Africa, a gathering is also necessary at this level in one form or another, to examine the religious problems which are raised for the whole continent, clearly in liaison with the universal church and the Holy See'.[8] In response to the request for a council expressed by the Africans, Pope John Paul II has just convened a 'Special Assembly for Africa of the

Synod of Bishops', which popular terminology is already calling the 'African Synod'.

The 1983 Code of Canon Law attaches various legal definitions to the expressions 'council' and 'synod' which it is worth recalling here. Canon law refers to two types of 'council': the ecumenical council (canons 337–341) – an assembly of the bishops of the whole church – and particular councils. These bring together above all the bishops of the same conferences of bishops or the same church province. As can be seen, the Code has not provided for a council of a continental type. But if the organization of an 'African council' thus strains canon law in its present state, it is worth saying straight away that the Roman Pontiff, who 'in virtue of his office enjoys supreme, full, immediate and universal ordinary power in the church, which he can always freely exercise' (canon 331), can ordain the celebration of an 'African council'.

The synod of bishops comprises two types of assemblies, general and special (canon 345). The general assemblies which deal with questions concerning the good of the whole church are either ordinary or extraordinary. The special assemblies (canon 345) are those which study the affairs proper to one or more regions.[9] The role of the synod of bishops is consultative, unless it has been given deliberative power by the Roman Pontiff (canon 343).

A French theologian, J. Levesque, has recently given his views on the status of the 'African synod'. Noting some phrases used by the pope about the preparation of this assembly, saying that the specific aim of the council of the General Secretariat of the Synod is to 'supervise the execution of what has been decided by the synod of bishops and approved by the Sovereign Pontiff', Fr Levesque draws a conclusion for the status of this assembly. 'Decided by the synod', 'approved by the Sovereign Pontiff': 'these are terms which seem to make the synod a deliberative organ and not just a consultative one,' he notes.[10] This remark would seem to me to be judicious, in that canon 343 stipulates that when the synod of bishops is given deliberative power, it must refer back to the Roman Pontiff for the ratification of its synodical decisions. Is it necessary to stress that the report of the discussions, deliberations and desires sent back to the pope at the end of the work of the synod prior to the redaction of the post-synodal apostolic exhortation bears the name 'propositions' and not 'decisions' when the synod is consultative?

Whether it is a matter of an African council, an African synod or another collegial authority, in all cases the delicate question of the articulation of personal episcopal power and collegial episcopal power surfaces again.[11]

The pope has returned on several occasions to the reciprocal limitations of the powers which guarantee the entire responsibility of each bishop in his diocese and the real legislative competence of the collegial authorities in making decisions.

Before ending this article, I would like to offer a few reflections. These lead me to speak of the major options for the episcopate of Zaire and to touch on the questions of patriarchate and primacy in Africa.

3. Some reflections

Two themes provide the framework for this series of brief reflections. One puts the Episcopal Conference of Zaire in the context of episcopal collegiality in Africa. The other discusses the question of patriarchate and primacy in Africa.

The episcopate of Zaire, one of the most dynamic in Africa, has time and again manifested its sense of collegial and pastoral responsibility in the intention that a truly African Christianity should arise at the heart of the continent. Vatican II has had a creative and dynamic reception. In welcoming the basic orientations of the council in an African context, the church of Zaire has gradually forged a new identity. In a 'Message to the Agents of Evangelization' in 1975, the bishops of Zaire affirmed the inculturation of the gospel and the Africanization of the church. Evangelization in depth in the sense of inculturation has always been the object of special attention on the part of the episcopate. The recent approval by Rome after more than a decade of experimentation of what is commonly called here the 'Zaire rite of the mass' is a point of no return in the course of inculturation and the creation of liturgies rooted in local cultures.

Other preoccupations of the episcopate of Zaire worth mentioning are the promotion of African theology, of which Zaire is already considered to be the cradle and the Catholic Faculties of Kinshasa are considered to be the melting pot, and concern with the family and the laity. The development of an adult Christian laity aware of its Christian responsibilities led Cardinal Malula to entrust certain parishes in Kinshasa to laity called 'Bakambi'.[12] As for African theology, the work of research and synthesis is already enormous.[13] Pope John-Paul recognized this in his address to the bishops of Zaire on their *ad limina* visit in 1983. He also recognized the relevance of African theology.[14] The bishops of Zaire have also worked out and published documents on human nature and the development of the country like 'All in solidarity, all responsible' (1977), 'Call for National Recovery' (1978) and 'Our faith in men and women, the image of God' (1981).[15]

There is no doubt that today the epsicopate of Zaire represents the rich pastoral experience of a church which is moving forward in the exercising of episcopal collegiality and teamwork round an authority favoured with a collegial spirit and shared responsibility – the Episcopal Conference of Zaire – which has led the bishops to go beyond the frontiers of their diocese and to feel themselves in solidarity with the one evangelistic mission of the church.

Through my reflections, I would also like to concentrate attention on a question which is constantly asked by those considering the future of Christianity in Africa: do we need a patriarchate or a primate in Africa?[16]

There is hardly any need to point out that the institution of the patriarchate, above all in the Eastern churches, has a history and traditions to which Africa cannot lay claim. To create a new patriarchate today would be artificial and anachronistic. For the true patriarchal churches that we know are matrices of faith which have given birth to daughter churches with which they have kept the same institutions, liturgical rites, traditions and church discipline over a long history. A patriarchate, even simply one of honour, would not make sense in Africa.

The title of primate, which is proper to the West, could be appropriate in Africa. In fact, in the Latin church this title does not imply any power of government. The Latin primates enjoy only honorary prerogatives (canon 438). This title of primate could be connected with a diocese of Uganda for the following reasons: it is the country of the first African martyrs, it is the country of the first black bishop of modern times,[17] and finally it is the country blessed by the first visit of a pope to the African continent.

Conclusion

Today we can say without any risk of deceiving ourselves that 'the African synod' will certainly take place. We warmly salute this courageous initiative of Pope John-Paul II in convening a special assembly of the synod of bishops for Africa. Since the plan for an African council has not been buried, in my view the 'African synod' is a step on the way towards an 'African council' which must materialize one day.

The brilliant theologian Mgr Philips, who will certainly not be regarded by anyone as a dangerous author, stated: 'At the council, the bishops do not sit as advisors of the Sovereign Pontiff nor as qualified informants coming from the four corners of the earth; as the old and venerable formula says, they are certainly "judges in matters of faith", pronouncing the verdict along with their president. In other words, as the formula used by

Paul VI puts it, the decisions are taken *synodaliter*, that is to say, by the Pope united with the fathers.'[18]

Notes

1. Mgr Philips lists no fewer than sixty titles relating to collegiality in his work *L'Église et son mystère au deuxième Concile du Vatican* 1, Paris 1967, 280–4.
2. From Sunday 27 to Thursday 31 July. Thirty-two cardinals, archbishops and bishops, representing the national and regional episcopal conferences of Africa, met for a symposium at the Pastoral Institute of East Africa-Gaba, about six miles from Kampala in Uganda. Cf. *Revue du Clergé africain* 24, 1969, 615.
3. The opening address by Cardinal Zoungrana is published in *Documentation catholique* 66, 1969, 860.
4. Ibid., 861.
5. 'Having acceded,' the Pope states, 'to the request made often and for a long time by Africans – bishops, priests, theologians and responsible lay people – that an organic pastoral solidarity should be promoted within the African continent and the adjacent islands, I have decided to convoke a special assembly of the synod of bishops for Africa . . .' (cf. *Telema* 2, 1989, 3).
6. For a more thorough understanding of the genesis and evolution of the idea of the 'African council', see Mgr T. Tshibangu, 'Un concile africain est-il opportun?', *Bulletin de Théologie Africain* 10, 1983, 165–73.
7. The interview given by the three African theologians of the special mission is published in the *Bulletin de Théologie Africaine* 10, 1983, pp.174–8. See also the account given by the Société Africaine de Culture of the meeting of the African theologians with the European public, in a stencilled memorandum, Paris 1981.
8. Tshibangu, 'Concile africain' (n.7), 169. In connection with a gathering of one form or another, J. Levesque reports that at Yaoundé the Pope used the term 'council', but in the plane on his way home indicated to journalists that he would prefer the term 'synod', cf. *Lettre Inter Églises* 51–52, January–June 1989, 4.
9. Current ecclesial language calls these three assemblies ordinary synods, extraordinary synods and special synods. So far seven general ordinary assemblies (ordinary synods) have been held (in 1967, 1971, 1974, 1977, 1980, 1983 and 1987); two general extraordinary assemblies (extraordinary synods, 1969, 1985); and two special assemblies (special synods: the Dutch Bishops in January 1980 and the Episcopate of the Ukrainian Rite in March 1980).
10. Cf. A. Ponce, 'Les enjeux du Synode Africain', in *La Croix l'Événement*, 15 September 1989, 20.
11. This has been brought out in particular by Cardinal J. Ratzinger, *Entretien sur la foi*, Paris 1985, 66f.: 'The clear restoration of the role of the bishop is in fact attenuated, to the point that there is a risk that he will find himself stifled by the integration of bishops in increasingly organized episcopal conferences, often given heavy bureaucratic structures. So the collective does not replace the person of the bishop, who is the doctor and the authentic master of the faith for believers entrusted to his care.'
12. There is already a modest bibliography on this pastoral experience: *Manuel du*

Mokambi wa Paroisse, Kinshasa 1975; A. Turck, 'Au Zaire; des paroisses officielle-ment confiées à des laïcs', in *Communautés et liturgies* 1, 1976, 32–7; Commission des Ministeres laïcs, *Role et fonctions du Mokambi de paroisse*, Archdiocese of Kinshasa 1985; Cardinal J. A. Malula, 'Le "Mokambi": un ministre laïc', in *Documentation catholique* 84, 1987, 1101f.; id., 'The Mokambi: Lay Men Responsile for Parishes', in *Origins* 17, 1987, 400.

13. The Seventeenth Kinshasha Theological Week on 'African Theology. Survey and Perspective', organized in April 1989, is part of the evidence of the harvest.

14. See *Documentation catholique* 80, 1983, 605–6.

15. For more details on these documents and the pastoral orientations of the episcopate of Zaire, see Mgr T. Tshibangu, 'L'évolution des thèmes des Assemblées des superieurs et évêques des missions catholiques au Zaire (de 1905–1979)', in *L'église catholique au Zaire. Un siècle de croissance (188–1980)*, Kinshasa 1981, 315–42; O. Bimwenyi K., 'Quelques options de la Conférence Episcopale du Zaire', in *Bulletin de Théologie Africaine* 10, 1983, 317–21.

16. After my contribution to the Seventeenth Kinshasha Theological Week in 1989 a delegate from Germany asked me what I thought of an autonomous patriarchate for Africa.

17. In 1953, Pope Pius said to Mgr Kiwanuka, the first African bishop, ordained in 1939: 'In you I am re-establishing the African hierarchy, interrupted centuries ago by the vandal invasions. . . . You must work energetically because it depends on your success whether I judge that I can consecrate new African bishops.' See *Informations catholiques Internationales* 260, 1966, 12.

18. Philips, *L'Église et son mystère* (n.1), 288.

Contributors

HERWI RIKHOF was born in Oldenzaal, Netherlands, in 1948. He studied theology in Utrecht and Oxford, gained his doctorate in 1981, was consecrated priest in 1983, and as a university lecturer is associated with the Theological Faculty of the Catholic University of Nijmegen, where he teaches dogmatics. His publications in the sphere of ecclesiology and Vatican II include *The Concept of Church* (1981); 'The Ecclesiologies of *Lumen Gentium*, the *Lex Ecclesiae Fundamentalis* and the Draft Code', *Concilium* 147, 54–63: 'De kerk als communio: een zinnig uitspraak?', *TvT* 23, 1983. 1, 39–59; 'Corpus Christi Mysticum. An Inquiry into Thomas Aquinas' Use of a Term', *Bijdragen* 37.2, 1976, 149–71; 'The Necessity of Church. An Exploration', *Archivio di Filosofia* 54, 1986, 481–500.

JAN GROOTAERS was born in 1921. A lay theologian, he was an observer at the Second Vatican Council and for the last twenty years has taught the course on 'Church and World' in the Faculty of Theology of the Catholic University of Louvain. He has written a number of studies on Vatican II and the synods of bishops, including *The 1980 Synod on the Role of the Family* (with J. Selling), Louvain 1983; he has also made an in-depth study of the Synod on the Laity, *Le chantier reste ouvert*, Paris 1988. He is now becoming Secretary of the Centre of Vatican II Studies in Louvain.

DONATO VALENTINI was born at Javre di Villa Rendena, Italy, in 1927. He graduated in philosophy in Padua and in theology in Rome. He was formerly Professor in Ecclesiology and Ecumenism and is now Director of the Institute of Dogmatic Theology at the Pontifical Salesian University, Rome. In 1987 he was visiting professor at the Graduate Theological Union, Berkeley, California. He is a member of the governing committee of the Italian Theological Association (ATI), and has been its secretary since September 1989. His main works are: *La teologia della storia nel pensiero di Jean Daniélou* (with a general bibliography from 1936 to 1968), Rome 1970; *Il nuovo Popolo di Dio in cammino. Punti nodali per una ecclesiologia attuale*, Rome 1984; he has also edited *Dialoghi ecumenici ufficiali. Bilanci e prospettive*, Rome 1983; *La teologia. Aspetti innovatori e loro incidenza sulla ecclesiologia e sulla mariologia*, Rome 1989.

REMIGIUS SOBAŃSKI was born in 1930 in Tarnovski Góry, Poland. A doctor of theology and a doctor of law, since 1958 he has been Professor of Church Law in the Priests' Seminary of the Diocese of Katowice and since 1971 Professor of the Theory of Church Law at the Canonistic Faculty of the Academy of Catholic Theology in Warsaw. Between 1981 and 1987 he was Rector of the Academy, and between 1976 and 1984 Consultor of the Congregation of Clergy. His main publications have appeared in *Prawo Kanoniczne*.

HEINER GROTE was born in Leipzig and studied Protestant theology in Leipzig, Bethel bei Bielefeld, Tübingen and Münster until 1963, after which he studied social history in Amsterdam and Tübingen, where he gained a theological doctorate in 1967. He is now a consultant at the Confessional Institute of the Evangelical Alliance in Bensheim, West Germany, and serves as a pastor of the Württemberg Protestant Landeskirche. In addition to publications on the social history of the nineteenth century he has written a good deal on confessionalism.

LUDWIG KAUFMANN was born in Zurich in 1918. After studying languages in Italy and England, in 1938 he entered the Jesuit novitiate, studying philosophy in the Canisianum in exile and theology in Lyons (1945–1949). He was engaged in the pastoral care of young people and in editorial work in Basel from 1951–1962 and was a reporter at the Second Vatican Council. In 1963 he joined the journal *Orientierung*, becoming its chief editor in 1973. His books include *Christenheit, Israel und Islam. Begegnung im Heiligen Land*, Lucerne 1964; *Damit wir morgen Christ sein können. Vorläufer im Glauben: Johannes XXIII, Charles de Foucauld, Kirchenkonflikt: Der Fall Pfürtner. Dokumente und zeitgeschichtliche Analysen*, Freiburg CH 1987.

PETER LEISCHING was born in Vienna in 1933, where he gained a Doctorate in Law in 1957; he qualified as a university teacher at the Faculty of Constitutional Law in the University of Vienna in 1964 with a work on the conferences of bishops. Since 1967 he has been Professor and Head of the Institute for Church Law and the Philosophy of Law in the

Law Faculty of the University of Innsbruck. His publications include *Der Ursprung der Leitungsgewalt in der Communio* (1972); *Kirche und Staat in den Rechstordnungen Europas* (1973); *Die römisch-katholische Kirche in Cisleithanien*, Die Habsburgermonarchie 1848–1918, Vol. IV (1985).

JOSEPH HAJJAR was born in Damascus in 1923 and ordained priest in Jerusalem in 1946. He is a member of the patriarchal clergy of the Greek Melkite Catholic Church. He has taught in universities and engaged in historical research. Among his publications are *Le Synode Permanent de l'Eglise byzantine, des origines au XI s.*, Rome 1962; *Le Vatican, la France et le catholicisme oriental. Diplomatie et Histoire de l'Église (1878–1914)*, Paris 1979; and the chapters on the Eastern churches in *Nouvelle Histoire de l'Eglise*, Vols. IV and V (from 1700 to the present). Since his retirement from academic life he has written a series of historical works under the general title *L'Europe et les destinées du Proche-Orient*: Vol. I, *Mohammad Ali d'Egypte et ses ambitions syro-ottomanes (1815–1848)*; Vol. II, *Napoléon III et visées orientales (1848–1879)* (two vols.); Vol. III, *Bismarck et ses menées orientales (1870–1882)* (two vols.), Damascus 1988, 1989.

PASQUALE COLELLA was born in Naples; a magistrate, he teaches canon law and institutions of public law in the University of Salerno, where he is also Director of the Institute of General Public Law. As well as contributing regularly to a variety of Italian legal journals, he is director of the journal *Il Tetto*; he has also published various articles, notably on 'Divorce' and 'Populus Dei', in legal encyclopaedias and symposia. He has also written *Il diritto di liberta religiosa nell ordinamento canonico*, Naples 1985.

THOMAS J. REESE SJ is a fellow of the Woodstock Theological Center at Georgetown University, Washington DC. He writes frequently for *America*, including coverage of meetings of the National Conference of Catholic Bishops. He is author of *Archbishop: Inside the Power Structure of the American Catholic Church* (1989), and editor of *Episcopal Conferences: Historical, Canonical and Theological Studies* (1989). He is working on a book on the National Conference of Catholic Bishops.

GERVÁSIO FERNANDES DE QUEIROGA was born on 19 June 1934 in Uiraúna, Paraíba, and ordained a Catholic priest on 26 July 1961. At the Gregorian University in Rome he did master's degrees in philosophy, pastoral theology and canon law, and a doctorate in canon law. He also obtained a BA in legal studies from the Federal University of Paraíba in Brazil. He is Professor of Ethics at the Federal University of Rio Grande do Norte in Natal and Professor of Ecclesiology and Canon Law at the major seminary in Natal, Rio Grande do Norte. He is a legal adviser to the Brazilian bishops' conference. His main published work is *Conferência Nacional dos Bispos do Brasil. Comunhão e Corresponsabilidade*, São Paulo 1977.

LUC DE FLEURQUIN was born in Schoten, Belgium, in 1944. After studying in Louvain and Rome he was ordained priest in 1972. Since 1975 he has taught at the Catholic University of Louvain and since 1977 in the Theological and Pastoral Centre of the Diocese of Antwerp. He is now Professor of Church Law at the Catholic University of Louvain. He was involved in the translation and final redaction of the Dutch text of the 1983 *Codex Iuris Canonica*. His publications have been on marriage law and church public law.

JULIO X. LABAYEN, OCD, is Bishop of the Prelature of Infanta, Philippines; Development Education Consultant to the Office for Human Development (FABC), Manila; National Director of the Socio-Pastoral Institute, Manila; and Board Chairman of the Asian Social Institute, Manila. He is responsible for statements at the plenary sessions of FABC, especially *Evangelization in Modern-Day Asia*, Teipei, Taiwan 1974; *Prayer – The Life of the Church of Asia*, Calcutta, India 1978; *The Church – A Community of Faith in Asia*, Sampran, Thailand 1982; *The Vocation and Mission of the Laity in the Church and in the World of Asia*, Tokyo, Japan 1986.

ANTOINE MATENKADI FINIFINI was born in Kinshasa, the capital of Zaire, in 1954. After studies there he was ordained priest in 1982 and then went on to St Paul University, Ottawa, Canada, for doctoral studies. He is now Professor at the John XXIII Major Seminary in Kinshasa, and at the Superior Institute of Religious Sciences and the Catholic Faculties there.

Members of the Advisory Committee for Ecclesiastical Institutions

Directors

James Provost	Washington DC	United States
Knut Walf	Nijmegen	The Netherlands

Members

John Barry	Edinburgh	Scotland
William Bassett	San Francisco	United States
Jean Bernhard	Strasbourg	France
Michael Breydy	Witten, Rhur	West Germany
Giovanni Cereti	Rome	Italy
James Coriden	Silver Spring Md	United States
Albertus Eysink	Zeist	The Netherlands
Antonio García y García	Salamanca	Spain
Jean Gaudemet	Paris	France
Thomas Green	Washington DC	United States
Joseph Hajjar	Damascus	Syria
Peter Huizing SJ	Nijemegen	The Netherlands
Ruud Huysmans	Voorburg	The Netherlands
Teodoro Jiménez Urresti	Toledo	Spain
Michel Legrain	Paris	France
Julio Manzanares	Salamanca	Spain
Elizabeth McDonough OP	Washington DC	United States
Francis Morrissey OM	Ottawa	Canada
Hubert Müller	Bonn	West Germany
Jean Passicos	Paris	France
Giovanni Rezác SJ	Rome	Italy
Reinhold Sebott SJ	Frankfurt am Main	West Germany
Remigiusz Sobański SJ	Warsaw	Poland
Robert Soullard OP	Brussels	Belgium
Luis Vela Sanchez SJ	Madrid	Spain
Francesco Zanchini	Rome	Italy

St Paul Publications

an activity of the Society of St Paul

MAKING FRIENDS WITH YOURSELF
by Leo P. Rock

In simple, non-technical language, the author identifies some of the reasons why we are not better friends with ourselves, and opens our eyes to marvel at God's goodness within us. **£5.95**

MAN'S ANGER AND GOD'S SILENCE
by Dermot Cox

A scholarly study of the Book of Job in an earnest attempt to answer the questions of suffering, injustice, alienation and the meaning of human life. **£5.95**

THE SPIRIT OF THE FATHER AND OF THE SON
by F.-X. Durrwell

A scholarly contribution to the century-old debate between Greek and Latin theologians on the relation of the Holy Spirit to the Father *and* the Son. **£4.50**

DAVID SINNER AND BELIEVER
by Carlo-Maria Martini

This book offers an inspiring portrait of David sketched by an innovative way of reading the Bible. **£7.95**

IN THE THICK OF HIS MINISTRY
by Carlo-Maria Martini

An authorative reflection on some passages of the Second Letter to the Corinthians enabling the reader to meet Paul in the midst of the daily grind and get a clearer understanding of what is happening in the life and work of those who have committed themselves to the service of the Gospel. **£3.95**

NO WAY OUT?
by Bernard Häring

Pastoral care of the divorced and remarried

"An eccellent work that deserves careful attention" *(Church Times)*. "A profoundly pastoral and compassionate book" *(The Universe)*. "To many pastors and many more people... it offers hope" *(The New Day Magazine)*. **£3.75**

A MAN CALLED JESUS
by Jean-Noël Bezançon

This faith-inspiring book leads the reader to a deeper understanding of the message and the mystery of Jesus. A book for every Christian who wants to rediscover the meaning of the life-giving words and gestures of Christ. A book for anyone "anxious to see Jesus". **£4.95**

PAULINE DISTRIBUTION SERVICES
St Paul's House, Middlegreen, SLOUGH SL3 6BT
Tel (0753) 20621 – Fax (0753) 74240